The Money Book
for Everyone Else

Also by Kelley Keehn

The Prosperity Factor for Kids
She Inc.
The Woman's Guide to Money

The Money Book for Everyone Else

Canada's Leading Financial Expert Tells You What You
Need to Know About Credit, Debt, Investing, and More

Kelley Keehn

with Lisa Bélanger

INSOMNIAC PRESS

Library and Archives Canada Cataloguing in Publication

Keehn, Kelley, 1975-
The money book for everyone else : Canada's Leading Financial Expert Tells You What You Need to Know About Credit, Debt, Investing, and More
/ Kelley Keehn.

ISBN 978-1-55483-019-0 trade paperback
ISBN 978-1-55483-039-8 ebook

1. Finance, Personal--Canada. I. Title.

HG179.K427 2011   332.02400971   C2011-900317-1

The publisher gratefully acknowledges the support of the Department of Canadian Heritage through the Book Publishing Industry Development Program.

Printed and bound in Canada

Insomniac Press
520 Princess Avenue,
London, Ontario, Canada, N6B 2B8
www.insomniacpress.com

Canada

DISCLAIMER

This book, in part, is designed to provide accurate and authoritative information on the subject of personal finances. While all of the stories and anecdotes described herein are based on true experiences, the names and situations have been altered to protect individual privacy. Neither the author nor the publisher is engaged in rendering legal, accounting, or other professional services by publishing this book. As a precaution, each individual situation should be addressed to an appropriate professional to ensure adequate evaluation and planning are applied. The author and publisher specifically disclaim any liability, loss, or risk that may be incurred as a consequence, directly or indirectly, of the use and application of any of the contents of this work.

The material in this book is intended as a general source of information only and should not be construed as offering specific tax, legal, financial, or investment advice. Every effort has been made to ensure that the material is correct at time of publication, but its accuracy or completeness cannot be guaranteed. Interest rates, market conditions, tax rulings, and other investment factors are subject to rapid change. Individuals should consult with their personal tax advisor, accountant, or legal professional before taking any action based upon the information contained in this book.

Very special thanks to:

Lisa Bélanger, Ph.D. student at the University of Alberta

Mark Dickey and the Alberta Securities Commission

To all those seeking financial independence through knowledge as a first step; I applaud you.

Simplify, simplify.
Henry David Thoreau

Table of Contents

Chapter Four: Avoiding Investment Schemes

Chapter Five: Tax Shelters

Chapter Six: Debt

Foreword

In the summer of 2009, I came to the brutal realization that the "Royal Bank of Dad" had closed a few years ago. I had just signed up for four more years of school and, like most 20-something women in Canada, I had a love/hate relationship with money. I loved to spend it, and I hated to save it. My father, CEO and founder of the Royal Bank of Dad, is an accountant and has always taught my sister and me the value of the dollar. Faced with living the next four years on a dismal income, I felt like I was looking into a financial black hole. That summer I started reading every financial book I could get my hands on to try to learn as much as I could, make the right decisions with the small amount of money I had, and try to make it work for me.

I came across Kelley's book *She Inc.*, which highlights the fact that money can equal independence and I couldn't agree more. Money may not buy happiness, but it can give the freedom to find happiness. This message was very empowering.

I, like so many people, desperately wanted freedom, but where to begin? In the next months I discussed this idea with friends, family, and people in the financial industry and one thing was clear: we are still not sure who to rely on for financial information. Our parents may or may not be financially savvy, our banker has an underlying agenda, and although throwing my money under my mattress was tempting, I realized that it might not be the best solution.

The objective of *The Money Book* is to give you the basics—enough information to make informed decisions and references to explore topics on your own. There are few relationships that will last throughout your entire life, but your relationship with money is one of them. From your first lemonade stand to your post-secondary education, merging assets in marriage, establishing a child's post-secondary education, and planning your retirement and estate, money is always there. Getting to know it may be one of the best ways to ensure a positive and prosperous relationship.

Knowledge is power. Money is power. A book teaching about money: priceless.

Lisa Bélanger

Preface

Since 2005, I have written six books. They delved into the psychology of money (*The Prosperity Factor* and *The Woman's Guide to Money*), practical money lessons for kids (*The Prosperity Factor for Kids*), and career and financial advice for women (*She Inc.*). Over those years, countless individuals (readers of my books and columns, people who saw or heard me on radio or TV, and those who approached me after one of my hundreds of lectures) have asked me to recommend "the" money book. Other than the timeless classic, the allegory of *The Wealthy Barber*, I couldn't really think of a book on the market that offered both the basics and the essentials on money. When my publisher called me and asked if I had another book in mind, we discussed the plethora of financial books on the market. We also agreed that there seems to have been a trend over the years to specialize financial books into advanced categories such as retirement and estate planning, succession planning, and more. We also noticed that the market lacked a uniquely Canadian book on the basics. This is that book.

More motivation to get this book out came with a nudge from Lisa Bélanger, main co-contributor on this project. Lisa contacted me over a year ago eager to get a book on the essentials out into the market.

The impetus, however, was years in the making and last year in the defining. During my twelve years in the financial industry, my career was mostly focused on affluent investors. Most might think, as did I, that those in the category of ultra-wealthy must also be ultra-knowledgeable in every aspect of finance. For most, that couldn't be further from the truth. I had many clients astute in various aspects of investing; yet everyone knew that they had more to learn. Of course, if it were not part of one's job, why would one be well versed in all matters money? To be sure, as a general rule, the more money someone has the more they've experienced financially and the more they generally know. This group tends to be the most eager for that knowledge, and they're keenly aware of the trials and tribulations of wealth creation. They want to do everything they can to continue to grow their riches while at the same time protecting them. I wish the same for you regardless of the size of your pool of funds. Furthermore, even the ultra-wealthy wish to impart financial wisdom to their children and grandchildren and aren't always able to articulate that knowledge.

This book was not written for either the wealthy or the financially challenged. It is a book for, I believe, everyone. There are times when you might face financial challenges, wonder about your credit, be curious about how to pay that mortgage off quicker, or need information about what investment best suits your risk profile and what documents you should have in place if (God forbid) something happened to you. Whether you have a billion in the bank or are a million in the hole, it's likely you have a number of financial questions. This book is written for Canadians seeking the essentials, the basics about debt, credit, investing, and how to choose a financial professional and avoid the fraudsters.

My hope is that after reading this book, and you may do so in one pass or use it as a reference guide as financial issues arise, you will feel protected and financially empowered. The financial world has become a frightening place full of Ponzi schemes and scams. The financial community itself can be confusing; I've taken on as many sides and presented all the biases (including my own) that I could fathom.

Some issues covered in this book might be familiar to you and other sections might be brand new. I don't know you personally and am not aware of your current financial circumstances. My intention is to follow the advice of Thoreau: to "simplify, simplify." And in the world of finance, it's the simple stuff that can be difficult for the average person to extract from the media.

I've learned a lot about what matters to Canadians, both from my experience sitting across from hundreds of clients in my work in the industry and from discussing what's on the hearts and minds of North Americans through the various media and speaking engagements. This book contains what I think everyone out there should know. There are a multitude of fantastic books on the market that delve deep into advanced financial concepts, however, this book is not that. It's just the essentials that I believe you need to know to lead a healthy financial life. I encourage you to move on to more advanced books if you find you have deeper questions after reading this. And if some information seems basic, please hang in there: I've assumed nothing and focused on simplification. It was at a workshop I was presenting to a group of high net worth investors where I learned to assume nothing. During that day, one woman asked me to explain what a GIC was (I thought it was common knowledge), but in the afternoon she asked me to clarify a question on flow-through-shares (a very, very complex and advanced question).

I thank you for investing your time with me and taking this step (which isn't always the easiest to do) for the sake of your financial life. Because so many websites change along with the financial information, rules, and new products, please visit www.kelleykeehn.com/themoneybook.html for more resources, articles, and calculators.

To your financial health and well-being!
Kelley Keehn

Chapter One

Credit

Quick Quiz

1. How many credit cards should you have?

A. Five

B. Two

C. One

D. None

2. Your mortgage payment history is listed on your credit report.

True ☐

False ☐

3. How often should you check your credit report?

A. Never—it hurts your score

B. Monthly

C. Every three to six months

D. At least once a year

4. You should have a low-limit card for making internet purchases.

True ☐

False ☐

5. If you have a poor credit score, there's not much you can do for six years.

True ☐

False ☐

Credit is the New Reality—Cash is No Longer King
I DON'T MAKE THE RULES—I JUST EXPLAIN THEM

The signs are everywhere—literally. Many merchants across Canada display signs apologizing that they can't accept $50 or $100 bills. In the spring of 2010, Air Canada officially announced that it would no long accept cash as payment for onboard purchases, only major credit cards. I was surprised to discover which cards are not classified as "major."

Recently, I was checking in at Toronto's Pearson airport and ran into a former colleague at the self-serve kiosk. He rarely travels, so after a few moments of catching up, I assisted him with the touch screen unit. He didn't have his itinerary handy and I told him to just swipe his credit card: by doing so, the system would find him and his flight. He pulled out his HBC MasterCard and to our shock, the message "Please insert a 'major' credit card" flashed across the screen. No, the machine wasn't broken. I had just used it with my "major" credit card and it worked fine.

We both learned a lesson. Not only is it essential to navigate our brave new world using credit cards (yes, we've officially been forced by the hotel, car, and airline industry to have one), but we must also make sure that the cards we do have are the "major" ones. I will explain later the differences between the various available cards.

As Canada moves forward to a cashless society (I think we're pretty much there), credit becomes a financial conduit impossible to avoid. Thus, I've started this book off with this essential subject, which is not only a taboo with friends and family but is also quite mysterious. How do you check your credit, and improve or maintain a good standing? What's on your credit report, what's not, and how do you fix something that shouldn't be there?

I fear that the outcasts and pariahs of the next decade will be those with poor credit. Those unable to secure a traditional (or major) credit card will be vulnerable to ridiculously high interest rates for the privilege of using other kinds of credit, if they can even obtain it at all. Of all the financial information I will share with you in this book, I hope you will read and absorb the information on credit. There's a stigma with credit and debt that there isn't in the rest of the financial world. We generally feel OK asking questions about investments, taxes, RRSPs, and other financial products. After all, the average person is not a financial expert and likely did not receive much if any education in high school or university about these concepts. However, as soon as we start asking our friends about credit scores and their ability to afford their debt (actually, these conversations rarely take place), the conversation shuts down. A person is unlikely to ask these questions of friends for fear of being financially "found out." And, most wouldn't dare ask their banker or creditor about credit and debt out of fear of appearing to be in financial trouble.

Even if you're financially sound, there's limited, candid information available about the nuances of the credit world: I hope to enlighten and empower you with *The Money Book*.

SOME DISCLOSURES

I must preface this chapter with a few things that I think are simply unfair. First, I think it's unjust that Canadians have to pay to find out our credit score. You can request a free credit report as often as you like, however, that report won't tell you your proprietary credit-worthiness score. If you're sitting with your banker for example and have authorized them to pull a credit report for a car loan, legally they aren't allowed to tell you your score. The reason? For the profit of the credit agencies, of course. Second, I don't think it is right that the two main credit reporting agencies in Canada are owned by American companies. The second largest, TransUnion, is owned by an American family. Third, the agencies and reports lack transparency and it's very difficult to get wrong information corrected in a timely fashion. And finally, many tips I'll outline to repair or maintain your credit score may seem counterintuitive. The credit agencies' proprietary methods of determining your score are not an exact science and you won't find specific strategies on their websites for increasing your score, how many points you lose or gain for certain actions (being late, closing accounts), and none of the calculations are done by a thinking, breathing human. Your credit score is determined by a computer- generated program that "assumes" many things. It's only through years of helping readers, viewers, and listeners repair their credit that I've learned the ins and outs of how to honestly and consistently keep your score positive.

I must also disclose a few of my own biases. I've known a few individuals who have purchased courses to improve their credit and absolve themselves of debt through methods that I feel are unethical. Some, but not all of these systems advocate practices such as avoiding creditors altogether, finding loopholes to not pay the creditor back, or to fight with the credit reporting agencies. If an individual signs their name to a piece of paper promising to pay back a loan, that paper should be worth something. And if they have to break that promise based on the terms of that agreement, they should do everything possible to honour it eventually. I'm not referring to debt consolidation. That's a valid practice where you get a loan, line of credit, or refinance your mortgage to then pay out all of your debts.

Credit Score Basics

So few Canadians have any idea what their credit score is or how it affects their debt. Credit is still a mystery to most and a societal taboo. But we need to start talking in order to dig our way out of this mess, especially with the current economic situation.

In early 2009, Credit Canada reported that Canadians were over $1.1 trillion in household debt. By December of 2009, the Certified General Accountants Association of Canada reported that the number swelled to $1.41 trillion and I'm sure that even as I write this sentence the number continues to rise.

You may be surprised that I didn't start *The Money Book* off by examining investments, the stock market, your mortgage, or some other instrument as the crux of your financial future. Think of your credit this way: It's much easier to build a brand new home than to fix a house that has a weak foundation, is full of mold, and is ready to fall apart. The same theory applies to your financial "house." It's easier to build than repair. If you have a great credit history, I want you to keep it that way. However, if your credit "house" is in need of a renovation or demolition, don't despair. With some discipline, courage, and a deep breath, your credit can be repaired.

If you have near perfect credit, then you're a part of only 5% of the Canadian population. So why would you need to care at all? First, you want to ensure that it stays strong and healthy. To do this, you must be aware of your credit rating and check it at least once a year, but I would recommend once every six months. Chances are, though, that if you are reading this, you're somewhere else in the 95 percentile.

There are three credit-reporting agencies in Canada and the two most widely used are TransUnion and Equifax. You can request a free credit report as often as you like, however, to get your FICO score (as explained shortly), you'll have to pay for that report on-line. With Equifax, for example, the full report with your score will cost around $24. When researching, be sure to visit the Canadian branches of the agencies, as both are also in the States. See www.transunion.ca and www.equifax.ca.

With today's prevalent internet and credit card fraud, you mustn't assume that all is well. Furthermore, most Canadians have not checked their credit report in the last year and many have never seen one at all. It is important to check that your credit hasn't been compromised; if it has, it's important to take quickly take action.

Even if you have no current need for credit, you should still pay attention to your credit score since many landlords and employers are looking for a great score. Not all employers in Canada will check your credit report, but the trend (commonplace in the US) is gaining momentum in Canada. Of course in Canada, your permission is needed for an employer to check your credit score.

INTERPRETING YOUR SCORE

Back in my old banking days, this score used to be an "R" rating. R1 was the best possible and R9 the worst. Today, the most common standard used by lenders is the FICO score. The acronym stands for Fair Isaac Corporation and it's a proprietary calculation.

Your credit score is a simply a snapshot of your current credit situation as well as your credit history over the past six years. Your credit score is an important factor in a lender's considering you "credit worthy" for future debt, consolidation, reduction of interest, etc. It's not your total picture. Your report *does not* factor in your employment status, cash flow, assets, net worth, or other important criteria a lender uses when deciding whether to approve or decline your request.

I'm not a lender and times have changed in Canada with borrowing becoming tighter due to the global recession. There is no magic score one should have, but the higher your credit score the better chance you have of receiving a loan. Of course, the other factors I mentioned are also important if you're seeking new credit.

The score range (with Equifax) is 300–900. Again, the higher your score the better. Only 5% of Canadians fall in the 850 or higher range. The majority of individuals (27%) fall within the 750–799 score range. Why does your score matter to a lender? It tells them, based on your past credit, repayment, late payments, etc., how likely you are to pay your future debts on time, late, file for bankruptcy, and so on. For example, history has shown that individuals with scores under 499 have a 78% chance of being delinquent in repaying their loans.

You might be asking what score you should have. Before the market meltdown in North America (in the early fall of 2008), a score of 640 was considered somewhat average, in that a lender would still consider approval if those other factors I mentioned were strong (job security, assets, net worth, etc.). However, given today's tighter lending, one should aim for a score in the 750 plus range.

If you find your score falling short of the 750 mark, you have some work to do. It takes time and regular good financial habits to increase your score, but it can be done. As you read through this chapter start to think about what your short-term and long-term goals could be. Create an action plan to improve your credit score and improve your finances. Just a little knowledge can go a long way.

WHAT'S ON YOUR CREDIT REPORT?

- Personal details pertaining to things like your employment history and your address. Basically, information that you gave to previous lenders.
- A detailed list of your current debts, including loans, and credit cards. This information is on your report for six years, so even if you've closed accounts, the information will still be there.
- Each debt listed will show the maximum credit limit and the current or last reported balance (most creditors today report monthly).
- If you've been late on your payments. Reports will show if and how many times you've been 30, 60, or 90 days late. These obviously hurt your score.
- If you're over limit on your account, if it's in default, paid in full, etc., this will show up on your account.
- If you've had an account go into default and it's been forwarded to a collection agency or the creditor's collections department, this will show in a section of your report.
- Banking information may or may not be included on your report.
- Public records and other information such as a bankruptcy or judgment against you will show up on your report.

CREDIT INQUIRIES

- An inquiry made by a creditor will automatically pull up three years of data going back from the date of the inquiry. The system will keep a minimum of five inquiries.
- These inquiries are also referred to as "hits" on your report and can bring down your score temporarily. There are "hard" and "soft" hits or inquiries on your report. For example, if you specifically apply for credit of some type, the lender will pull your report, registering a hit/inquiry on your report. If you do

this with several lenders in a short period of time, your score can be pulled down since it might appear that you're "seeking" credit, which can be a red flag to lenders that you're "in need." Mark Twain once said, "A banker is a fellow who lends you his umbrella when the sun is shining, but wants it back the minute it begins to rain." A lender, of course, doesn't want the risk of lending to anyone who is desperate: They only want strong candidates. You might have innocently been shopping around for a new car or mortgage, however, those "hits" raise more questions for the last lender, such as: Why didn't you get approved the first few times? Were you declined by the first few lenders? If you can't get credit elsewhere, why should the last company you approach extend credit? It's only one factor in pulling down your score, but it does show that you should not seek credit in a short period of time with many lenders.

- If you are seeking the best rate on a loan or don't know for sure if you'd be approved with a lender, pull your report yourself and bring it to your meeting with you. (It does not affect your score if you check your own report—it shows as a soft hit.) If the lender approves you, they'll still need to pull your report and register a "hit," however, if you weren't going to stand a chance of being approved, they'll generally let you know and you'll save having another inquiry on your report that could pull down your score further.

- Soft hits or inquiries on your report will show, but do not affect your score. These are hits from things like you pulling your own report or existing creditors taking a peek at your report to see if they'd like to perhaps increase your limit. If you read the fine print when you accept a loan or credit card, you'll see that the lender asks permission to periodically check your credit (likely to see if they should increase your credit card limit later for example). These are your soft hits/inquiries.

WHAT'S NOT ON YOUR REPORT

In Canada, generally, your mortgage is not on your credit report. This is shocking to many Americans since it's on their report. Many Americans (and Canadians) wonder how we build our credit standing without our largest debt being reported. There may be instances where your mortgage could be reported, such as a second mortgage or one that's with a non-Schedule I bank (one that's not in the "Big Six") or if it's structured as a secured line of credit, but I haven't seen the latter. Check your personal report to verify whether your mortgage appears. Generally speaking, if you have a conventional mortgage, it will not show on your report. Therefore, if you've always been diligent in making your mortgage payments on time but have been a little lax with your credit card minimums and loan repayments, you might find your score less than favourable since you won't have your good mortgage payments to offset it.

Utilities, depending on the province and type (cell phone bills might show up), are not on your report. However, if you don't pay your cable bill (even if it's less than $50) for example and it goes into collections, this could show up in the collections section of your report and will dramatically pull down your score.

If you order the full enchilada as I recommended earlier from either Equifax Canada or TransUnion Canada, you'll find the reports are quite detailed, well laid out, and easy to read. Also, if there's something on your report that is wrong or shouldn't be there at all, both agencies have dispute resolution instructions on their site.

Cleaning Up Your Credit

Before reading this section, take the time to review your own credit report. Here are some tips to improve your score over time if you've found that it's less than favourable. Remember, your score is fluid. A great or poor score today can change next month and for the better or worse. You can change your score dramatically with a year's worth of positive or negative habits. Here are some guidelines to follow when trying to improve your score:

- *Always make your minimum payments on time.* Sounds simple and self-evident, but many individuals miss their minimum payments periodically, which can drastically pull down their score. To avoid making this mistake, enter your debt payment due dates on your calendar as a reminder. Making a payment even one day late can register a blemish on your report, which will stay there for six years. If you're over 60 or 90 days past due, this will bring down your score significantly. And if you're paying your credit card using online banking, make sure you do so at least three business days before the due date if the credit card is with a bank other than the one you deal with. If you bank with BMO for example and your credit card is with Scotiabank, make sure there's enough time for the online payment to be processed. If you bank with BMO and your credit card is also with them, you can simply transfer funds online the same day.

- *Pay more than you're required.* If you're maxed out on your credit cards, pay more than your minimum payment. You never want to be "over limit" on your cards, as this too will significantly pull down your score. For instance, if one of your cards has a credit limit of $3,000 and you're right at the maximum, paying the $120 minimum payment requested by your credit card company will likely not cover your interest due at the statement date (this is also the date your company will report to the credit agencies). Let's assume the interest on your card is actually $140: This would put you $20 over limit right at the time they report to the credit agencies. Furthermore, you must budget for your annual fee, insurance protection, etc. I know it may surprise you that not every credit card company will ask you to pay your minimum payment plus your over limit amount. Some will keep letting the account be over limit each month. The major credit cards (remember that when I say "major" credit card I'm talking about a VISA or MasterCard with your bank) will ask for the minimum payment plus any over limit amount or fees to bring the account back under the credit limit. However, some credit cards count on account holders being over limit each month so they can ding them with an "over limit" fee.

- *Keep your balances low.* Ideally, you should not have more than 75% used of your card's limit. For example, if you have a credit card with a credit limit of $10,000, keep that balance under $7,500, ideally at 50% or less. If you find yourself continuing to carry a balance, you'd be better to spread that balance over two $10,000 limit credit cards. The reporting agencies do factor in total dollars used in credit, total available credit (even if they're all zero balance), but most importantly, they view your ratio of available credit to the balance used. Obviously, the higher the percentage, the more it will lower your score, since it makes you look like you're not being responsible with their credit or that they might be in trouble.

- *Don't seek new credit if you're trying to improve your score.* The worst thing you can do if your score is low is to seek new credit, which is a sign of possible trouble.

- *Get rid of high interest credit and department store cards.* Not all debt is viewed equally. Two department store cards would be less favourably viewed than two traditional VISA or MasterCard accounts and could thus have a negative impact on your score. Because a department store card is easier to be approved for than a conventional credit card and even if there's a zero balance, the credit agency wonders why anyone would keep a card with such a high rates.

If you find that you have a number of debts with high interest rates, you may wish to speak with your banker about a consolidation loan. Consolidation loans pay off all your higher rate cards with a low rate, forcing you to pay a set amount and pay down the principal, costing much less over time. However, if your score is low, talk to your banker first about the likelihood of their approving such a loan before they pull your credit report.

If you need to rebuild trust with your banker and/or reestablish positive credit habits on your report, consider a cash-secured loan. In a cash-secured loan you'd provide, say, $1,000 and the bank would lend you $1,000. The point is to show a positive repayment history and thus build up your score or a cash-secured credit card. You may wonder why you need credit if you have cash. In this situation you don't "need" credit, however, it would be prudent to use your cash to rebuild your credit for the future.

Wrapping up this section on credit, here are a few of the most commonly asked questions I've received over the past couple of years.

Q#1: If I have a credit card with my spouse. I'm building credit, right?

A: Likely not. If your spouse has a credit card and has ordered a supplementary card on their account, you don't have to be approved as an individual. Even if you both have separate cards with unique card numbers on each, they still may be linked back to one account. You can easily find out if this is the case on the monthly credit card statement. Your spouse would be responsible for your spending and the paying back of the debt. Your purchasing would still form part of their overall account limits, credit standing, and ability to apply for loans. The basic rule is that if you didn't have to "apply" for the credit, then you're not building credit in your name. Consider if your spouse were to, God forbid, pass away or separate from you, this credit extension and card would disappear as well.

If you're the main cardholder of a credit card, you can get a supplementary card for almost anyone—your spouse, your child (maybe if they were travelling abroad), your assistant, etc.

Q#2: How do I build credit?

A: If you're seeking some type of lending with no credit history, it can be as challenging as if you were someone with poor or less than perfect credit. Using the example above, the spouse with the supplementary card (not their own card or account) could use that card to apply for, say, a department store card. I NEVER recommend this strategy generally, but sometimes it's the simplest path when building credit, if done responsibly. If you have a credit card of any type, most department stores will automatically approve you for one of their cards with a low limit—perhaps $300. Once you get this card, be diligent in purchasing small items from the store that you likely need at some point anyway and *immediately* pay them off, right at the store. Never carry a balance on these cards, as their rates are generally very high. Once you've done this for a few months, perhaps as long as six months if you have no balance at all, you'll find they'll generally increase your credit limit. This is a good first step. Today, many department store cards in Canada are also tied to a MasterCard. With one client of mine, after the individual followed my recommendations with his responsible use of his department store card (a limit of $300) he was offered a regular MasterCard with a limit of $3,500 in less than one year.

Remember my earlier story of the fellow trying to use the kiosk at the Toronto airport? It was a department store MasterCard that he was trying to use and it was not considered a major credit card. Having a major credit card is essential when travelling today. To build your credit, once you have a department store credit card and have had a year or two of positive credit activity, I would recommend trying to get a bank credit card. Bank credit cards are "major" credit cards and more difficult to be approved for due to tighter requirements. With a bank VISA or MasterCard, you need a higher credit score and income to qualify, as opposed to an equal limit department store card (i.e., a $2,000 limit bank credit card and a $2,000 non bank credit card such as a HBC MasterCard or Capital One Master Card). Herein lies one of the reasons why the department store card charges more interest—they're taking on riskier clients than the bank would.

Lastly, consider cash-secured loans and credit cards as mentioned earlier. The cash-secured card won't be considered a major credit card, but it can be a great tool for building a positive credit score.

Q#3: Should I get my child/adult child a credit card to help them build credit?

A: As with the first question, if you choose to give your child, spouse, or someone else a supplementary card to then assist them to apply for a department store card, please keep in mind that you are still on the hook for the supplementary card. Are they responsible enough to stick to your rules for purchases? If not, consider that you, solely, are held accountable for covering all purchases made on any card or supplementary cards on your account. If you do completely trust your child, you may wish to have your bank or credit card company give you a low limit (say $500) credit card and get the supplementary card on that account. That way, if you were wrong about your child's spending habits, the most you'd be out is $500, as opposed to more from some of the much higher limit products available.

With this strategy, remember, they're still not building credit with the supplementary card. You're simply getting them one so they can then get a card of their own (as mentioned in the previous question) and then you could cancel their supplementary card on your account.

The last time I spoke with VISA and MasterCard, they told me there is no age requirement for a parent wanting to get a supplementary card for their child. While I'm not a proponent of getting your child a credit card, it might make sense to give your child a supplemental card if they are travelling overseas on a trip or leaving to school for an extended period. Instead of possibly having to wire money to your child, you could get them a supplementary card as an emergency option.

Q#4: If I get all those credit card offers in the mail telling me I'm pre-approved for $10,000, $50,000 or more, I must have good credit, right?

A: No, not necessarily. Credit card companies, unless you already have an account with them, cannot access your credit report. That would be an invasion of your privacy if you have not authorized them to do so. These card companies are *assuming* you have good credit based on your postal code or some other list. Or, perhaps it's simply a numbers game for them: mail out enough of these offers and someone will actually apply. Always, always read the fine print. There you'll usually see a magic annual income needed for that approval along with a long list of other disclaimers and approval requirements.

Q#5: Suze Orman says to pay yourself before you pay your credit card payment—is this a wise thing to do? I heard Suze Orman (American Financial Guru) say on her show that viewers in financial trouble should pay themselves first (save what they would pay on their credit card) before they even pay their credit card payments, even if it means their score will dramatically decline. Is this a wise thing to do? (This question came in late 2008 when the financial crisis was talked about on all the airwaves in the US and Canada.)

A: First, Suze is an *American* Financial Guru. One must realize that the Canadian and American banking and financial systems are almost like night and day in most respects. The banking system has been hit much harder in the US. Since they have very little regulation down south, many financial institutions operated like the Wild West—it was shocking to read the media reports of how little regulation the American banking and financial system had in place before the recent crisis.

According to a statistic I heard on CNBC's *On The Money*, as of late 2008, over 62% of American credit card holders had their credit card limits reduced (forced upon them) or closed entirely by the issuer (during the crisis), so I can see why Suze would make such a recommendation. Technically, because a credit card is revolving and a "demand" loan by the lender, a credit card company is well within their right (even though it's not common practice in Canada) to close a person's account at any time. If someone were facing financial difficulties and paid their credit card diligently but had no savings for themselves, and then the issuer, out of the blue, cancelled their credit card (demanding full payment), it might be prudent to have some emergency cash savings. After all, survival at that point would be more important than worrying about a credit score that could later be fixed.

However, in Canada, we're not facing the same dilemma as our neighbours to the south. Sure, credit's a bit tighter here, but we're on solid footing. Actually, the IMF (International Monetary Fund) has ranked Canada as the strongest banking system in the world. I've also spoken to the Canadian Bankers Association, the banks, and credit card companies and they tell me it's business as usual. They haven't suspended or closed credit card accounts due to the recession.

A point of interest to be aware of is that even if the credit card companies in Canada are not following what their US counterparts are doing and closing out credit card accounts, legally they are allowed to do so. A credit card works like a demand loan—the operative word being "demand." According to the fine print when you signed up for your card, the company can technically demand payment in full at any time.

So having a solid slush fund of three to six months' savings (equivalent to your income) is always prudent, however, in our country, I would not recommend missing any credit card payments in order to boost a savings account; our system is pretty stable. Furthermore, one missed credit card payment can haunt your credit report for years and pull your score down dramatically. Plus, if you were paying double-digit interest rates on your card, it wouldn't make sense to throw your money into a savings account paying a dismal rate of return.

(Even though I answered this question in January of 2009, much of what was happening in the US is still plaguing the population. Experts aren't unanimous on whether the crisis is over or when it will start to ease, let alone recover. Be cautious when listening to media reports about the economy, banking, and finance, as the US system is dramatically different from ours.)

Q#6: If I exercise the "skip a mortgage" payment option, will this affect my credit score?

A: No. This is an option that many Schedule I banks offer (i.e., the big banks such as TD, RBC, Scotia). Today, if you bank online, you can even apply to exercise the option immediately. However, it's still at the discretion of your lender. You can only skip a payment once a year and remember you're now paying compound interest over the term of your mortgage by refinancing that skipped payment. Be cautious about skipping a payment and do so only when you really need to.

But as long as you haven't "missed" a payment, are on time with your payments, and don't have any amounts in arrears, this would not affect your credit rating.

Tip Stop

Remember, most Canadians don't realize that their mortgage payments are not included on their credit report, so ensure that your loan and credit card payments are always on time and in good order. Your diligence in paying your mortgage is great, but won't help bring up your credit score.

Q#7: I called my credit card company and asked them to reduce my interest rate. Will this affect my score? I was surprised that they were willing to negotiate and did in fact drop my rate as asked. After I hung up, I wondered if they'd see this as a sign of financial weakness? I can pay my bills and am not having troubles with debt—I simply wanted a better rate. But will this affect my credit score?

A: No, it won't affect your credit score. For it to do that, you'd need to be late with a payment, over limit on your account, or in default or nonpayment.

You really did do the right thing and most people are surprised that they can negotiate with their bank or credit card company. More often than not, when asked to lower an interest rate, a bank or credit card company will agree.

Give it a try and start negotiating yourself. Ask for the annual fee to be waived, a reduction in your credit card rate, mortgage/loan rate, and more. A simple question could save you hundreds or even thousands of dollars!

Q#8: Why did my score drop when I closed out two accounts? I had an excellent credit score of over 800 and have always paid my bills on time. I closed out two credit card accounts, as I didn't need them anymore and hadn't used them in some time. Then, to my shock, I found out that my credit score dropped down to about 740. Why did this happen?

A: The credit reporting agencies are vague with answers to questions like this. There are no specific criteria (that I know of, anyway) that tell how much your score will go up or down based on closing accounts, opening accounts, etc.

However, yes, unfortunately, one's score will temporarily drop when closing an account. Why? I don't have the answer. This is the craziness of the credit reporting agencies and the credit card companies. The man who asked the question above found out from the credit card company that his score would indeed drop by closing the account. His question was, "Why didn't they tell me this before I closed the account?"

When your score is being determined, all of your accounts are factored in. Having two credit card accounts with a zero balance is actually a good thing. Do not close these accounts. If you find that you're not using them, put the credit card in a safety deposit box, use it once a quarter and pay off the entire balance immediately, just to keep it in good standing and to continue to have positive reporting on your account. Check if the card has an annual fee. If you're not using the account regularly and do have a high annual fee (such as a points/reward card), switch it to a no fee or low fee option.

My suggestion if your accounts have been closed anyway and your score has dropped is to consider taking out a new credit card. Initially, your score will likely drop slightly by doing this, but within a few months of keeping a zero balance (but using it regularly and paying it off) it will bounce back.

I don't make the rules and I do take issue with them when it comes to the credit reporting agencies and financial practices of the credit card companies. Mostly, I don't like the limited amount of information and education on their practices that is available to the general public.

Q#9: How do I dispute something on my report?

A: You can dispute or make a comment on your credit report directly with Equifax or TransUnion. See their website for instructions. If something has been wrongly reported, you may wish to contact the company that incorrectly reported to the bureaus and ask them for a letter stating the reported information was incorrect. If you're applying for credit while this process is in place (it can take up to six months to have something corrected on your file), obtaining a letter directly from the company that reported the incorrect information will generally suffice for most lenders.

Q#10: How many credit cards should you have?

A: As discussed previously, don't accept credit card offers in the mail, over the phone, at the airport, or in a department store. Limit the number of cards you have and ensure you carefully read the annual costs and other hidden fees for the cards you do have. I suggest you have at least two credit cards, preferably one major VISA and one major MasterCard. Plus, ensure you always have one card with a zero balance (if possible) for emergencies.

Q#11: OK, I'm in trouble. What should I do? Is there hope for me or do I have to seek bankruptcy?

Bankruptcy is a legal process by which individuals or businesses seeking government protection from creditors when the borrower is unable to repay the debt owed. Although bankruptcy may sound like a good option, it is a serious process that one should not enter into lightly. The trust of a lender or service provider is broken when all payments cease. To be absolved of this responsibility can potentially have damaging consequences for one's self-esteem. In the past, I had counselled a number of clients who had no option but to file for bankruptcy. The blows to their self-esteem were long sustained, not to mention the negative impact bankruptcy had on their ability to borrow in the future. What I was surprised to learn was that the clients who were least emotionally bruised were the ones who were slowly paying back their creditors, even though they didn't need to and weren't required to do so in their bankruptcy agreement. Honouring their commitments was important to them. Although their insolvency afforded them a second chance, they took responsibility for keeping their promises.

I neither support the process of bankruptcy nor condemn those who fall prey to overeager credit providers or unfortunate life circumstances. What I am saying is that bankruptcy should be considered a LAST RESORT. If this path seems like your only option, consider the impact that bankruptcy can have on your emotions and credit before you initiate the process. Furthermore, many bankruptcy trustees fail to mention that once you file, a number of careers are automatically closed to you, including those in the financial industry.

It is important to note that not all debt would be discharged. For example, you cannot be absolved of your student loans and child support payments.

Before declaring bankruptcy, first figure out where you are. You might not be in as much trouble as you think. So many individuals file bankruptcy for small amounts of debt.

Second, what assets do you have? Are you able to consolidate your debts with your bank thereby reducing your interest costs and monthly payments? Depending on your situation, you could cut your costs in as much as half by fixing your high interest rate credit card debt to a mortgage (assuming you have equity in your home).

Consult your banker, financial planner, or the credit counselling agencies in your specific province (head to www.kelleykeehn. com/themoneybook.html for a list of resources) before visiting a bankruptcy trustee.

You may wish to go directly to your creditors for help. Most do not want you to default on your agreements and will usually work with you, especially if your cash flow situation is temporary. If you have a gold credit card and your balance never seems to be paid off, your bank might have a lower rate credit card that you can switch to or a loan with a much lower rate and forced principal re-payment options.

There are costs associated with bankruptcy that depend on your income, assets, and other factors. Bankruptcy is not simply walking away debt free (unless you have a very low income and no assets), there are trustee fees that vary from province to province, and each province has a fee for filing bankruptcy which needs to be paid by the individual filing for bankruptcy or by liquidating their assets.

Lastly, although there are many ethical bankruptcy trustees out there, their bias is generally towards that end. A good friend of mine was in very serious financial trouble about fifteen year ago. He was encouraged not only by trustees to file for bankruptcy, but also by his friends and family. Everyone told him that his credit and situation was so severe that bankruptcy would absolve him of his debt repayment requirements and his score would improve quicker than trying to repair it himself. But for him, it was a matter of pride and honour and he vowed he wouldn't break his promises to those he owed money.

At times, his situation was so bad that his car and his wife's minivan (that they needed to drive their kids to school with) were repossessed. His business phones were disconnected due to lack of payment and he owed the government gobs of money. Almost every dollar he brought in was garnished for the taxes he owed. His wife later confided that there were times that she'd only have $2 to put in their car for gas and prayed that the car wouldn't stall getting the kids to school.

I watched my friend struggle for over a decade (he had struggled for many years before we met). He'd get ahead slightly and then some major financial catastrophe (some very much his fault and some not) would blindside him. But he was never derailed from his determination to clean up his credit and become debt free.

Today, nearly three decades later, he appears to many to be an overnight success. He has two multimillion-dollar companies and is personally debt free. The very companies that were cutting him off financially now beg for his business.

Would my friend have been better to simply file for bankruptcy and have a fresh start decades sooner? The simple answer is yes. But would he really have been better off? Many trustees and counsellors I have chatted with share the sad statistic that many they counsel never got the second chance message and in fact were on their second, third, and even fourth bankruptcy.

When choosing someone to talk to about potential bankruptcy it is a good idea to first go to www.creditcounsellingcanada.ca and find a list of credit counsellors in your area. Once you have some choices, contact the Better Business Bureau to ensure they are a reputable counsellor and ask if they are for profit or not-for-profit.

Check out my website for some fantastic budgeting worksheets at www.kelleykeehn.com/themoneybook.html

Q#12: I've had something recently go to collections. Will that show up on my credit report?

It may or may not. If you have a collection agency contacting you, it's in your best interest to clear this up as quickly as possible. Simply ask the agency if they've already reported the occurrence on your credit report. Many won't if you act swiftly. And ensure that you keep excellent records of your payments. Some companies have been known to try to re-collect years later, leaving you to prove that you've paid the outstanding amount. Even if you're in the right, it may take you some time to remover such an error from your credit report.

Q#13: How long does something stay on my report?

Six years in most provinces.

Q#14: Are there times when I should establish credit even if I don't need it?

Remember the Mark Twain quotation? It's paramount that you apply and secure sufficient credit while your financial situation is solid (if possible). Although I cautioned earlier about taking on too many credit card accounts, there is a delicate balance between too many and not enough.

Here's an example. You've been employed by your current company for some years. Your general financial picture is solid. You decide to leave your company and open your own business (or perhaps leave to have more children). Six months into your business, after not receiving a salary, you realize that you really could use an operating line of credit to get you through that tough first year in business. Now when you apply for credit, the lender will look at your current income (which is none in this example), see that you're on a new, perhaps risky venture and your employment history will not be fully considered. Many in this instance would not be approved without collateral or some other strength.

Ideally, in the above example, if you knew you were leaving your stable career as an employee, you would apply for a line of credit before you left that position. However, should you need it later, when your financial situation is less stable, it will be there for you without the need to apply for it.

Case Study—Ethan

WHERE ONE PERSON WAS AND WHERE HE QUICKLY WENT.

The following is a credit case study on an individual I'll refer to as Ethan, which of course is not his real name. Ethan came to me for help in 2004 and has agreed for me to use his information and situation as a case study (provided his name was changed and his situation described generically).

Ethan was in severe need of credit counselling and was one small step away from bankruptcy, but within a relatively short period of time he turned his financial future around.

When Ethan first came to see me, the business he had recently opened was struggling relentlessly. He jokingly commented on several occasions that his receptionist worked one third of the hours he did and was taking home twice the pay. Each month, his financial situation worsened. He used one credit card to pay the minimum payment on another, was behind 30–90 days on every one of his loans and most days, didn't have the courage to even check his bank accounts and how many NSF (non-sufficient fee) charges were going through. He didn't know if there would ever be a way out.

The following is a chronological look at how Ethan rebuilt his credit, life, and financial self-esteem, step by step.

FEBRUARY 1, 2004

Ethan knew he was in trouble. He just didn't know how bad it was. He also knew he should pull a credit report, but didn't have the courage on his own. With a little figurative hand holding and a deep breath, we ordered an online report. The news wasn't great. To give you an idea of how brutal his situation was, it was only when Ethan filed his 2004 taxes that he realized that he had incurred over $1,700 in NSF charges for the year.

Score on February 1, 2004: 530

It could have been worse, but at 530, things were bad. According to Equifax Canada, only 4% of the population has a score as low as this. At that score, 60% will default on a loan, file for bankruptcy, or fall 90 days past due. The only group score worse than Ethan's is that of 490 or less: that group constitutes 78% of all delinquencies. Ethan was certainly, not the ideal candidate for a consolidation loan with a major bank. Ethan had even applied for the highest rate credit card offered to him weeks before coming to see me, hoping to use it to pay current monthly bills, but his application was declined. His sheer willpower and vow to never declare bankruptcy kept him focused on the financial repairs he needed to make.

HIS SITUATION IN 2004

Ethan wasn't quite ready to pack up his business and throw in the towel. He had sunk every dollar he had into his company, spent 70–80 hours a week for the past two years trying to make a go of it, and desperately hoped things would turn around.

He had three credit cards with maxed out balances of $7,900, $2,900 and $650. The startling issue with the last card was that his limit was $250 but the total balance owing was $650. How is this possible? Some cards, and usually non-traditional bank credit cards, have many hidden fees. Since Ethan was continually late with his payments and the monthly interest and penalty fees kept adding up, the card with the $250 limit's balance nearly tripled.

One of his bank-issued cards had some surprising fine print as well. Ethan's annual interest rate was 18%. However, as we were carefully reading his most recent statement, there was a small paragraph that stated that since he had a history of not making his minimum payments on time, his current annual interest rate had increased to 24%. Until he made his minimum payment on time for at least six months, his annual rate wouldn't drop back down to 18% again.

Ethan's other personal debts included:
- A car leased at $480 per month
- Two loans with a small lender at 28% interest with monthly payments of $800
- A first mortgage with a Schedule I bank
- A second mortgage with a private lender with payments of $250 per month
- No department store credit cards, collection on his credit report, bankruptcy or other major blemishes

Other factors affecting his score:
- Credit card one: two payments more than 30 days late
- Credit card two: no late payments, but over limit
- Credit card three: late payments, which have pushed the card over limit
- Loan one: four 30-day-late payments and one 60-day-late payment
- Various past credit (loans and credit cards) paid off, up to date, and no further reported late payments.

A macro recap of Ethan's situation and credit score are thus: The number of current late payments, over limit situations on his credit cards, and the number of current debts have all brought Ethan's score near to the worst possible.

At this point, he was seeking help, but really needed to know where and how severe the situation was. He was barely keeping his business afloat and had no idea how he was going to pull himself out of his situation. His company was not making enough for him to cover his personal monthly obligations, let alone that of his business.

Despite my advice, Ethan decided not to do anything at that

moment. He had a number of emotional issues that meant he couldn't act.

NOVEMBER 2005

Ethan came back to see me with his updated credit score. He hadn't done much financially since the last time I'd seen him. His company was still struggling, as was he personally. However, he was much more aware of his situation, and trying to pay his debts on time, but with a cash flow that was sketchy at best, he was still juggling which bills would be paid and which ones not each month.

What was different for Ethan this time was that he had opened a second business that was starting to produce a profit. He was very committed to turning his life and financial future around and seriously wants to do whatever it took to improve his score and fate.

Ethan had a home with considerable equity in it, but since his score has been undesirable to lenders and his income over the past year was near nil, no Schedule I bank wanted to consider lending to him based on that equity. Since he couldn't magically change the fact that his income was near nothing, the only thing he could do was improve his score. His goal was to obtain a new mortgage in the spring of 2006 and consolidate all of his debts, if possible.

Score in November 2005: 653

At this point, his score had improved slightly from his situation in 2004. He still had a number of current late payments and two of his credit cards were still over limit, but he hadn't been seeking credit, which is good, and his hard hits were all fairly old.

At a score of 653, Ethan was in the 11% FICO score range. The delinquency rate for the group range 650-699 was still 23%, therefore a conventional lender would still likely consider him a high risk and limit his options for new credit or a consolidation loan, which he was so desperately seeking at this point.

JANUARY 2006

Score in January 2006: 658

Ethan was really trying at this point. His score hadn't moved up much at all since November. He wanted his next batch of scores to be over 699. He worked hard to keep his balances under the maximum and had even gone as far as to swallow his pride and borrow a few hundred dollars from family members to ensure he paid his minimum payments on time.

FEBRUARY 2006

Ethan finally made contact with a lender at a Schedule I bank. The lender wasn't thrilled with Ethan's lack of reported income over the previous three years or the number of late payments on his credit history. However, with the amount of equity in his home and the recent climb in his credit rating, his lender was willing to try.

Ethan had hoped to obtain a mortgage for approximately 75% of the value of his home, which was still a conventional mortgage not requiring him to obtain CMHC insurance. (Today, you need only 20% as a down payment to avoid paying CMHC fees. We'll examine that in depth in the debt chapter.) His goal was to acquire enough financing that he could pay off all of his debts and perhaps receive a little more to renovate his home or invest in the stock market.

For Ethan to fully pay off all of his high interest rate debt, he would need a mortgage of about 60% of the value of his home. At the time of his application with the bank, they were only willing to lend him up to 50% of the appraised value. Although somewhat disappointed that he wasn't able to pay off all of his debts, Ethan was thrilled that he would be able to pay off his extremely high interest debts. The mortgage counsellor also informed him that if he took care of his credit over the next six months and improved his score, he could likely come back and obtain a line of credit. As far as I know, Ethan did just that.

MARCH 2006—MY LAST VISIT WITH ETHAN

Score in March 2006: 723

As you can imagine, Ethan was simply thrilled with his new score. In just over a year, and with a reasonable amount of effort and minimal pain, he was able to take his score from one considered unsavoury by the lending industry to one that made him a viable candidate for a loan. By paying down and eliminating many of his loans, credit cards, and the second mortgage, his score jumped considerably in just one month. At this score, Ethan shares his spot with 32% of the population. His score is still below average, however, many lenders would consider this satisfactory. The delinquency rate for those residing in this score range (700–749) is only 5%.

Ethan vowed to never again purchase more than he can afford, fail to meet his minimum monthly obligations, or allow his business to push him further into debt.

Ethan's story was originally featured in my book, *She Inc.* I was curious to see if Ethan had kept up his vow for financial freedom or had he fallen back to his old ways? I spoke with Ethan in January of 2011 and he's still slowly working to pay off his debt, but is thrilled to report that his outlook on money and spending has changed dramatically. He told me that he spent a great deal of time examining his old ways of spending on credit and making impulse buys. Today he still feels the occasional need for "stuff" that he can't afford, but he's made a promise to himself since we last spoke that he'd wait 24 hours before making any impulse buy (which he says he does and has saved himself considerable dollars by practicing this). He's bringing in extra income renting out his basement and regularly tweaks his budget by taking an in depth look at his spending twice a year.

Mistakes to Avoid

MADISON: READ THE FINE PRINT

Madison is a very bright young woman finishing her Ph.D. Like many of us, she's overtaxed from working while finishing her doctoral studies and is guilty of not always reading the fine print. Madison was moving from B.C. where her family lives to attend school in Ontario. Before she left home, she needed a laptop for school, but, of course, didn't have the money to pay for it. She was shopping at a local office supply store and the sales attendant informed her of their store credit card offer. The sales person told her that she could get a laptop that day with no interest and no payments for six months as long as she paid with their credit card. Delighted, Madison left with her new computer.

A few weeks later, Madison headed to school in Ontario. Shortly after, Madison's dad called to let her know that the first letter for her laptop purchase had come in from the office supply store. She told him not to worry about it (and not to open it—she didn't want him to see how much she spent on the laptop) and that she had a no interest, no payment deal for six months. Each month though, her worried dad would give her a ring when this envelope came in the mail and with each call, she reassured him.

Several months later, Madison wanted to change cell phone providers. She filled out the application and to her shock she was declined. She was completely baffled about how it was possible since her credit card and student loan payments were on time every month. When she went home to check her credit score, she found out that it was a frighteningly low score under 500 and the account on her laptop was sitting in collections.

After a few phone calls she found out a critical piece of information that the sales person had neglected to tell her. The store credit card actually offered six months *interest* free, not *payment* free. The mistake ruined Madison's credit, and she'll be repairing it for the next six years, simply because she didn't read the fine print. Lesson to learn: never trust what anyone says a document states without actually reading every word of it yourself. If you don't fully understand or agree with any clause, don't sign it!

LIAM: BEING JUST A LITTLE LATE CAN COST BIG BUCKS

Liam always pays his credit card's minimum payment each month, but somehow, he's always just a few days late. He always finds a reason for not getting to the bank in time to make his minimum credit card payment each month or forgets when he pays it online to factor in the three business days required for the payment to make it to the credit card company on time. One day, he brought all of his financial statements to me and asked if he could be doing something better with his situation.

While sifting through his papers, and specifically his credit card statement, there was a small sentence at the bottom of his credit card statement's front page that read: "Until you make six months of consecutive minimum payments on your account, you will be charged 29% interest." Because Liam was chronically late making his payments over the past year, he had been paying an interest rate of 29%, not the 18.5% (which is high enough) that he thought he was paying. Because he was late and failed to read his credit card statement each month, he missed a huge red flag and money was wasted over the years.

Let's crunch the numbers: Assuming Liam actually paid his credit card on time, but only paid the minimum payment:

Balance: $9,200.00
Original interest rate: 18.5%
Minimum payment: $276 monthly (3% of the outstanding balance)

Assuming he locked his credit card in the freezer in ice and doesn't make any new purchases until it's paid off, it would take Liam (ready for this?), 18 years and 4 months to pay off his credit card and he would pay an additional $8,736.83 in interest.

If Liam committed to paying his monthly minimum payment each and every month plus an extra $44 a month (so, his payment would now be $320 instead of the required $276), he would pay his credit card off in just three years and two months and only pay $2,799.00 in interest—a savings of just about $6,000 and it would take him 15 fewer years to pay it. Just by paying on time and upping his payment a measly $44 a month (just over a $1 a day)!

The real scenario:

If Liam had never come to me and kept paying his minimum payment late each month, he would have continued being subject to a 29% annual interest rate. Look at how the numbers change if he had only made the minimum payments at this rate:

It would have taken him 38 years and 8 months to pay off the card, plus he'd have paid an additional $31,127.80 in interest. Even if Liam didn't make any extra payments over the minimum, his not paying attention to the increased interest rate being charged could have cost him an additional $22,000 and added an extra 20 years of making payments.

DANTE: FIGHT, BUT STILL MAKE PAYMENTS

Dante returned his luxury car, which he leased, when the contract still had six months to go. When he returned it, the dealer determined that the car hadn't been properly serviced over the years, there was a little more wear and tear than his contract allowed, and that he was over on the allowable kilometres, and therefore the car's residual value was less than was estimated in the original lease agreement. Dante was furious and when the dealer wouldn't budge, he stormed out of the dealership. But why should he care? He returned the car; it was their problem now.

He called the carmaker's head office and the client care representative said that they would work with him to resolve the issue. Phone calls went back and forth with the dealer and head office. Months passed and the issue still had not been settled. Dante thought nothing of it; he was on top of the situation, as far as he knew.

Three months passed and it was time for Dante to renew his mortgage. He has a great relationship with his bank and earns a pretty decent income, but because he's self-employed, he finds it is still a challenge to get approved for financing. But, when he met with his banker, Dante was told that his application was declined. Dante had been diligent in paying all his debts on time. When he was told about his low credit score, he didn't believe it.

What happened? Well, the dealership put the amount owing on Dante's lease into collections and since Dante was still on the hook for the last six months' payments, his credit report showed him four months in arrears (this is a huge blow to a credit score). The fact that it was in collections also greatly brought down his score. If Dante had come to an agreement and settlement when he brought his leased car back to the dealership, he would have been done with his agreement. Although Dante (and everyone for that matter) had the right to fight a contract or debt obligation he felt was unfair, he still should have made his minimum payments each month. Fair or not, the credit bureau doesn't know about the dispute you're having. Dante would have been better to keep making the minimum payment and try to recoup that money later on from the dealer, rather than ruin his score and try to get that off his credit report later on. Dante will eventually be able to get the car payments out of collections, but the hit to his score for not paying for four months will be detrimental and will show on his report for the next six years.

ZAIRA: DOING EVERYTHING RIGHT, BUT...

Zaira is the perfect example of handling credit responsibly. Not only does she pay her credit card on time every month, but she pays the full balance each month too. It irks her to pay one cent in interest. When Zaira finally got around to checking her credit report for the first time, however, she discovered that she had a very mediocre score. How could this be when she not only pays her card each month, but pays it in full? She also has two loans—a car and student loan—both of which are up to date and paid each month on time.

It's possible that Zaira is carrying too much debt on the loans or that when the bureau adds up her available credit, it still calculates her as having too much "credit." (Keep in mind that if she has, say, $20,000 limits on her credit cards, even though she keeps a zero balance on them, the "non-thinking credit bureau" factors in that she *could* max them out at any time.)

A second and very important possibility is that she's not aware that the credit card companies report your balance at the "statement date," not the due date. I personally have three credit cards—one has the same due and statement date—the other two do not. It is generally the norm, not the exception, that a credit card will have a different statement and due date.

Let's use Zaira's situation to illustrate:

- November 15, 2010—The date that Zaira's credit card statement for the month of November is issued. (Look at the top left or right on most statements to find the date.) This statement tells her the minimum payment due (even though she pays everything off each month) and the due date of December 8, 2010.
- December 16, 2010—Zaira's billing date for her December

statement stating that her new minimum payment is due by January 8, 2011 and so on.

• Here's what happened in December.

   • December 6, Zaira goes to her bank and pays her credit card off in full.

   • That's perfect—a zero balance with days to spare before it's due, therefore, Zaira pays no interest.

   • On December 14, the installers of her hardwood floor arrive and she decides to pay them with her credit card for the points. Her available credit on her one card is $10,000 and the hardwood bill is $9,200—perfect!

   • Zaira goes about her life not thinking about her credit card balance because she knows she has until early January to pay it off in full before she's subject to interest costs.

The Problem: December 16 is the date that her credit card company reports to the credit reporting agencies. So, if Zaira makes a major or even significant purchase each month before the statement date, it will bring her score down even though she has until early January to pay it off. Most consumers are shaken when they find out this information about the actual date balances are reported.

So what is the lesson? Make note of two dates in your calendar for each credit card. One: the due date for you to pay off the entire balance to avoid interest costs or at least to make your minimum payment on time. And second, the statement date (if different) and ensure the balance on this date is as low as possible. Don't make major purchases before the statement date. If you're close to being maxed out, remember, the statement date is also when the interest is applied to your account. If you're carrying a balance, this could tip you over limit. You don't have to keep track of the statement date if you're not concerned about your score or if you never make a large purchase (or rarely do) each month and pay your balance off. But, if you do carry a balance and are trying to repair your credit, it would serve you to keep careful track of both.

A question I received from a participant at a recent workshop was, "Wouldn't the credit bureau know that you were paying your balance off every month even if you happened to run it up at statement date?" The answer is no. If your credit card company just reports your balance once a month and that happens to be on the statement date (and perhaps, when you have a high balance), then no, paying off your credit card in full each month will not be captured for the sake of your credit score.

BROCK: THE MINIMUM ISN'T ENOUGH WHEN YOU'RE AT MAXIMUM

Brock is maxed out on his one department store credit card. He's making the monthly minimum payment requested and on time, but the problem is, he's maxed out and paying dearly for it.

> Credit limit: $3,500.00
> Interest rate: 29.9%
> Statement date: October 23, 2010
> Minimum monthly payment: $126.00 due on November 18, 2010

Here's the problem. Brock pays the minimum of $126, but he also has his monthly gym membership coming through on this credit card. On his last statement date in October, the finance charge (the interest due) on this account was $91.92. Basically, since Brock is always maxed, he can estimate what the interest will be and adjust what his credit card company is asking him to pay and pay more. His gym membership is for $48.28 each month. Add that charge to his finance charge and Brock has $140.20 worth of additional charges on his card this month. If he pays the requested minimum payment of $126 he's short only $15.80, but his credit card company allows his membership fee to go through, instead of declining him. For that convenience he's paying an extra $29 each and every month he's over limit (called an over-limit fee). Because Brock has been doing this for close to eight months without paying attention (and his credit card company still asks for the same minimum amount allowing him to go over limit each and every month), his current balance is actually sitting at $3,759.81. That's right; he's racked up $259.81 in over limit fees alone. Not only is this crazy (had he not gone $15.80 over limit each month, he'd have the $260 in his pocket), but it's also hurting his credit score every month.

For Brock to avoid being over limit, his next payment should be:

The minimum of $126.00 + the $259.81 he's currently over limit + his gym membership fee + a cushion (ideally of a few hundred dollars—keeping in mind the annual fee that will eventually be due as well).

Because the credit card company only asked for a certain amount to be paid, Brock is paying heavily. Lessons learned: read your statements carefully, do the math, and even if you can't get out of a jam in one month, a few extra dollars here and there allocated to your credit card balance will eventually get you on the right track. Plus, in Brock's case, he should examine how much that gym membership is actually costing in interest and fees and consider cancelling it and opting for some no cost running and a few weights around the house!

Tip Stop

If you find yourself in a situation like Brock's where your card is at the max each month, call your credit card company and tell them that you never want them to allow a purchase to go through which puts you over limit. (Allowing you to go over is a practice usually done by department store credit cards and non-bank VISA and MasterCards—bank obtained credit cards usually won't let you go over limit as easily as the others, but they still do.) The credit card companies will try to sell you on the notion that they're doing you a favour by allowing you to go over limit, but they're not. Not only do they charge exorbitant interest rates, but the over limit fee is usually much higher than the amount they'll let go through.

Recap

- Credit has become necessary to function, travel, and exist for most of us in today's environment.
- Be selective when choosing credit cards, loans, and other sources of credit—read the fine print!
- Limit the number of credit cards you have, but ensure you carry more than one.
- Delinquencies can stay on your credit report for six years.
- Become familiar with your credit report and check it at least once a year.
- If you find yourself in trouble with debt and are unable to make ends meet, seek help from a reputable credit agency.

See my website (www.kelleykeehn.com/themoneybook.html) for a list of budgeting resources, credit counselling agencies in Canada, and more.

Chapter Two

Protecting Your Financial Life

Quick Quiz

1. You don't need to review your credit card statements with VISA and MasterCard because you're 100% protected against fraudulent purchases.

True ❑

False ❑

2. If fraud occurs with your debit card, you're not protected.

True ❑

False ❑

3. It's a good idea not to have savings accounts with large amounts linked to your debit card.

True ❑

False ❑

4. Identity theft isn't much of an issue here in Canada.

True ❑

False ❑

5. When paying with your credit card, there's nothing wrong with showing your ID when a merchant asks.

True ❑

False ❑

Credit Card Theft

I was researching a piece I was doing for CBC National Radio on credit and debit card theft. One of the producers I was talking with mentioned a thoughtful call she had received from her banker. Her banker told her that she should have a low-limit credit card ($500 maximum) in addition to her high-limit card (with a limit around $10,000). Her banker suggested that she use the low-limit card for suspect purchases, such as those on the internet or at locations that seemed to raise an eyebrow.

This seemed to be a considerate, proactive conversation initiated by the banker. And these conversations seem to be catching steam across Canada: I hear more and more credit card holders "protecting themselves" by pairing low-limit cards to those with a high limit (usually their points cards). However, you are in fact fully protected by VISA and MasterCard in the event of the theft or loss of your card. Even if you are still in possession of your physical card and the thief has obtained your information in some other way, for example online, you will still be covered. I've spoken to the official spokespeople for both VISA and MasterCard and no matter the amount; you're fully, 100% protected against loss.

So why the attentive call from the banker? Consider that thieves are becoming better and better at stealing our credit card information, while at the same time Canadians know that they're protected and so carefully comb through their monthly statements for fraudulent charges. Who's on the hook for fraudulent activity and recouping those costs if we the consumers, are off the hook? It's actually the credit card companies and the banks who are left covering the deficit. Also, innocent merchants often end up absorbing the cost.

Should you have a low-limit card for suspect purchases? Sure, if you'd like. But remember, it's not necessary. In the early days of purchasing from the internet, I did exactly that and got a low-limit card (I think it was around $1,000). I used it only for online purchasing and when having to give my card details over the phone. It was stolen a few times and one purchase was for $1,500 USD. I found it curious that if I had tried to purchase something for amount that I would have been declined, yet, the fraudster's purchase was allowed to go through.

SOMETIMES CASH STILL IS KING

I know that in Chapter One I implied that cash is dead, but it's not. Cash is essential extra protection in today's plastic reliant society. What would happen if all of the credit and debit machines all went down one day (God forbid)?

After a long, gruelling workday there's nothing that will spoil a shopping experience as much as hearing the dreaded "declined" when paying for a purchase. Recently, while using my debit card for a relatively small purchase, my card was declined. Shocked and dismayed, I mumbled my disbelief. While a long line of irritated customers sighed, I insisted the clerk retry my card—it failed me when I needed it. Annoyed with myself that I didn't have more than five dollars cash in my wallet, I defaulted to my credit card. Knowing there was a large amount of funds in the savings account I was trying to access, I tried again at another store and still heard the dreaded word "declined" from the store clerk.

I called the number on the back of my card and they informed me that my "card was compromised" and my limit for purchases had been reduced to $200. When I pressed for an explanation as to why, the call centre representative simply repeated the statement and told me I had to go to my bank branch to get a new card. Easy for him, since he wasn't the one working during banking hours making it impossible for me to get a new card that week. Plus, I was shooting a TV show in Toronto. Furthermore, the purchases I was trying to make were both under $200.

Lesson learned: because we're "protected" from fraud on our debit and credit cards, these companies and the banks are flagging accounts quicker than ever and shutting down access or reducing limits much quicker. Without a debit card and no time off to get to my bank, I, of course, had no ability to access cash either. Thank goodness I had two back up credit cards to make it until my next day off. Ensure that you have at least two credit cards and that, ideally, both have a zero balance.

Take a moment today and ensure that you have a reasonable amount of cash on hand that could take you through a long weekend. I recommend you keep at least that amount somewhere in your home and a minimum of $100 cash in your wallet. A great trick I employ is to keep $100 Canadian and $100 US money tucked away in my wallet. The American money is pretty much at par with ours as I write this today, but somehow I never seem to spend it (I do have to replenish the $100 Canadian though, quite frequently).

WHAT HAPPENS WHEN A FRAUDULENT PURCHASE IS MADE ON YOUR ACCOUNT?

First, you need to pay attention to your credit card statements each month or better yet, review them every few days online. This is especially necessary if you and your spouse share the same account since it's pretty difficult to remember every purchase when the statement comes in a month later. Not only is it essential to check your statements regularly to avoid fraud and being over charged by your credit card company, it can also allow for an early warning that your identity has been stolen. Having your identity stolen is a much bigger problem than having your credit card stolen: we'll examine the difference shortly.

If you do find a purchase on your credit card statement that's fraudulent, contact your credit card company immediately. Once you've called your credit card company, depending on the size of the fraudulent purchase in question, they may or may not send out a form in the mail (usually an affidavit) and have you swear that the purchase was not made by you. What the credit card company will then do is go to the merchant to see if the purchase made was done over the phone, via the internet, or in person with your signature (if so, they will send you a different form so you can validate if that it is not your signature). One other thing to consider in the process is, depending on the relationship you have with your bank and/or credit card company, they may or may not release the hold on your available credit until everything has been cleared up. It may not even be fraudulent. I once checked into a hotel that accidently put an $8,000 hold on my credit card for my three nights' stay instead of the correct amount of $800. I only discovered the error when that credit card was declined for a purchase. My credit card company and the hotel corrected the problem, but it took three days for the hold to be lifted. Again, it's essential that you carry more than one credit card and that at least one of your cards at all times has a zero balance for just such occurrences.

THE PROTECTION IS GETTING TIGHTER

Not for you and me, but for the credit card companies. Since they're ultimately on the hook for fraudulent purchases, it's in their best interest to monitor the types of purchases you make, the places you make them most, and to shut down the use of your card if even the most minor of red flags pops up. It is a good idea to notify your credit card company if you are travelling, especially out of the country. You can imagine the hassle if you card is cancelled when you are abroad.

My mom has had her "high-limit" card since the 1970s. She's never maxed it out (not even close) and has proudly never paid a cent of interest, as she's always paid it off on time. The words "your card has been declined" are ones she's never heard in her life. Unfortunately for her, she was out having lunch with a friend and wanted to pick up the bill only to hear those dreaded words from the server. Horrified and confused, her friend covered the bill since my mom only had her VISA. Certain it was some glitch with that restaurant, she decided to get a few groceries on her way home and was declined again. When she got home the mystery was solved. There was a voicemail from VISA letting her know that there was some unusual activity on her account (turned out to be two gas purchases out of province) and for "her" protection, they cancelled her card. Doesn't sound so bad, however, it took 14 business days for my mom to get a new card in the mail. Imagine if she had been travelling with no other credit card? Or, imagine if that were you and, for not fault of your own, you were doing some last-minute, yet oh so important and essential Christmas Eve shopping, and your card was flagged? What would you do? Would you have the cash to cover your purchase? If you were out of town, how would you check into a hotel or book a flight change, as both require a major credit card?

I should note that depending on the nature of the suspicious purchase, the credit card company will either fully cancel your card (and send you a new one) or just flag your card. (In the latter instance, you can simply call your credit card company and confirm that the purchase was indeed made by you.) For example, I once left my regular high-limit card at home and only had my back up, zero balance, emergency credit card with me. As I don't use it often, my history of purchases is limited with that card. I happened to make a large purchase (near the limit) and my card was declined. I called the credit card company and they immediately released the hold and allowed me to use the card again, however, it was an inconvenience as it meant another trip to the store. (Had I known that all it would take was a call to solve the problem, I would have simply called from the store to release the hold.)

Although you are fully protected from purchases that weren't made by you, you should do your best to safeguard your credit cards and, as mentioned, have at least one clean card with no balance for emergencies. If you have two cards and your main card is put on hold, you'll have a second card, ideally at a zero balance, as a backup. To further prevent but not necessarily avoid such situations, give your credit card company a call before you travel or when you're about to make a large or unusual purchase.

Debit Card Fraud: How Does it Differ?

You are now protected from fraud when using your debit card as well. Just a few years ago though, it was much more difficult to dispute a debit card fraud than one on your VISA or MasterCard. To protect your cash from being preyed on, you might consider unlinking bank accounts with higher balances from your debit card cards. Let's say you have three accounts—your day-to-day banking, a chequing account, and a savings account. You should make sure that if you have a large amount in your savings or other accounts, you disconnect them from your debit card, meaning that you can't access those accounts with your debit card. If you do need the funds, you can easily transfer them online while still protecting your high balance accounts from debit-card fraud.

Identity Theft vs. Credit Card Theft

As discussed, having your credit card stolen or limited in any way, shape, or form is inconvenient or at the most, embarrassing, however, having your identity stolen can be devastating.

Your identity is everything you've worked so hard to accomplish: your great credit score, your reputation, and your relationships. Losing your identity can cost you years of hard work, money, time, and can lead to so much hassle. It also can affect many aspects of your life for years to come. You should strive to do everything that you can to protect your identity and if something does get stolen, act on it immediately. This section highlights some very simple things you can do day to day to save your precious identity.

Don't show your ID when making purchases

This request is becoming more widespread and its implications, although seemingly innocent, could put you at risk for identity theft. Years ago when I was in Kelowna, a store clerk asked to see some ID when I paid with my credit card. Curious about this request, I asked why. The lovely clerk replied, "If your credit card was stolen, wouldn't you want a store to check for ID so it could be caught?"

That answer was logical and most considerate. A store looking after my well-being? How fantastic! As I travel the country for business frequently, I've witnessed this trend catching on in every province. This practice started to bother me, however, when I watched a news report detailing some thieves who had set up cameras in a number of stores to record shoppers' debit card numbers and PINs as they innocently paid for purchases—some in major stores. We've all heard reports of these things happening across Canada from pay-at-the-pump gas purchases to covert data skimming at some ATMs and at major retail outlets.

For your protection or theirs?

I contacted VISA and MasterCard for their comments on the practice of merchants' requesting ID at the cash, since the merchant agreement clearly states that all that is necessary for a consumer to pay with their credit card is a valid card (as long as it hasn't expired, the signature at the back is legible, etc.). MasterCard said that presenting your valid card was enough to fulfill the purchase. VISA also agreed but prefaced their statement by saying that there are times they support merchants' asking for ID on select items, such as with electronics, but, that a store could not routinely ask for ID with every purchase.

If someone steals your card or number without stealing the physical card, you're still protected. Sure, it's a massive inconvenience, but you won't be held financially responsible. Having all of the information stolen from say your driver's licence, however, certainly could have very serious implications. Imagine if the store clerk innocently asks for your ID and there's a hidden camera recording your credit card number, the expiry, and your name on the card. Whip out your divers licence and the crooks now have your full name, driver's licence, date of birth, and full mailing address—just about everything needed to fully steal your identity (and in many cases, this information would be enough). The only other piece of information that someone trying to steal you identity would be after would be your social insurance number.

A store may not refuse your purchase with a credit card if you decide not to show your ID. I have, on a number of occasions, been refused and although I explained all of this to the store clerk and manager (OK, argued) they still refused my purchase with a credit card. In all cases, I have reported these stores to VISA/MasterCard. Bottom line: A store is allowed to *ask* you to provide ID as a store policy, but you are not *required* to do so by VISA or MasterCard, which is clearly stated in their merchant account agreement.

What are your options?

So, you have a few choices: not to show your ID, not to shop at the stores that required you to show your ID, or simply to use cash or a debit card. If none of these are convenient, invest in some Wite-Out tape. You can find some at your local office supply store for a few dollars. Simply apply the tape (which is only tacky—so it won't permanently adhere to your licence) to all of your information except your name and signature—that should be the only thing your store clerk or even airline needs.

Times are changing with the advent of chip cards and machines, which bypass the need for a signature and ID. However, until every store has one of these, keep your personal information to yourself and protect it even during busy shopping times, like the flurry of the holiday season.

Enjoy your day-to-day shopping, but please do so with care. That clerk may really believe she's protecting you by asking to check your ID or her manager may require her to do so, but protect yourself. Keep your identity safe even if it holds up the line.

DON'T CARRY MORE THAN YOU NEED

Check your wallet and purse when you head out and make sure that you carry only what you need. Leave your passport, SIN card, health care card, and more at home. I reflect on the number of tragic stories I've been told of those who have had a full purse or wallet stolen and it's haunted them for years to come. My friend's mother had her identity info packed purse stolen 20 years ago. Since then, fraudsters over the years have used her character for everything from applying for credit to impersonating her for employment. She's on constant alert with the credit reporting agencies and has to monitor her financial life relentlessly. Head out with your credit and debit card, some cash, and your driver's licence—that's it!

MAKE A LIST OF YOUR BILLS

Given how stretched for time all of us are, would you notice if one of your bills didn't show up? Most Canadians wouldn't miss seeing a credit card statement that didn't arrive on time. Actually, many might hope the bill just disappeared altogether. But that can be the first sign that something is wrong. Make a list of all of your bills and their approximate arrival dates, especially if you're travelling. You might think a fraudster getting their hands on your bills is no big deal, but, it's a first red flag that someone might be diverting your mail to their address; they may be applying for new credit or changing yours. If they're now receiving your mail, you wouldn't know if they applied for a new credit card in your name. Plus, some mail such as government papers contains important information, such as your social insurance number, that gives thieves more ammunition to apply for credit in your name.

INSTALL A MAIL SLOT

To ensure that you and only you get your mail, install a slot that drops mail right inside your house if possible.

SET UP EXTRA CREDIT CARD PASSWORDS

Call your credit card company and set up an extra password on your account in addition to the "secret" one, which usually defaults to your mother's maiden name. If a trickster had that information and got hold of your card, they could change your address, apply for new credit, and more without your knowing about it. Just ensure it's a password that you'll never forget or you might have difficulties accessing your own account in the future when calling in.

NEVER LET OTHERS HEAR YOUR SECRETS

Victims of financial crime often report that the culprit was someone very close to them. Never make a call to your bank or credit card company and allow anyone to overhear your secret pass-word—not a spouse, friend, or colleague.

BE WARY OF EMAILS

Most of us who have been using email for some time are quite aware of the phishing scams that arrive in our inboxes daily. How-ever, as the spammers get more creative, it's sometimes difficult to spot these nefarious missives. If you're somewhat new to email, phishing emails are "fishing" for your information. They might look like a credible bank email asking you to click "here" and make a password change for example. They will then store your password to use for their own purposes later on. A bank will *never* email you to ask for your password.

I recently had an email from Facebook informing me that my account had been hacked leading to its being suspended. I almost responded to it. The only thing that stopped me was that the email came in on my regular account and my Facebook emails are linked only to my Gmail account. During a busy time of year, you may have opened a new bank account or signed up to PayPal and all of a sudden, you get an email from that company the next day. The scammers are working on pure numbers. They know that on any given day, a person might have opened a new RBC or Scotiabank account, Facebook, PayPal, or more. Then, during the busyness of an unsuspecting email user's day, when an email comes in from what appears to be one of those companies, the recipient thinks nothing of it because they just opened an account with them. The email scammer is counting on that person to innocently click on their link and hand over their information. Remember that no cred-ible financial institution or service will email you requesting a re-sponse via email. Even if the email address says that it's from your financial institution or other company you deal with, don't believe it. And if you're still in doubt if the website is the right one, give your bank a call and ask them to verify their online banking or merchant site.

CHECK YOUR STATEMENTS

Do you pore over your monthly statements with a fine-toothed comb? If you're like most, probably not, especially if you and your spouse use the same card. If that's the case, create a central location for receipts that you can reconcile at the end of the month. Who remembers that $20 purchase from an unusual merchant weeks later?

Recently, I discovered my credit card number was compromised, but barely noticed it. After reading my statement, a curious charge of $25 showed up three times. Had it been once I might have ignored it, but the third time was the charm. I called up my credit card company and it turned out that someone in another province had purchased three calling cards using my credit card number. When in doubt, give your credit card company a call. Even small purchases could be a tip off that your number has been stolen.

SOME FINAL TIPS FOR PROTECTING YOURSELF FROM IDENTITY THEFT:

- Get a secure internet network at home that's password protected.
- Install spyware on your computer.
- Delete your cookies and temporary internet folder often and always sign out of a secure website such as your bank, PayPal, etc.
- Shred it if it has your name, address, or even an account number on it. When in doubt, shred or burn documents in your fireplace, don't toss them out.
- Don't keep your SIN or passwords on your mobile devices such as cell phones, PDAs, and laptops; they're easily lost or stolen.
- Don't post personal information on social networking sites such as your home address, phone numbers, or birthday (including

year).

- Download the latest patches and fixes to your computer to avoid vulnerabilities.
- Install a good virus protection software.

If you suspect you've been a victim of identity theft, contact the RCMP, your bank, and the credit reporting agencies (see Chapter One) immediately.

Recap

- Make a list of your bills and check it twice. Be sure to read through them thoroughly and that all purchases are correct. You don't have to wait for your credit and bank statements to arrive in the mail. Check them often online. It's difficult to reconcile every purchase for the month by the time the statements come in.
- Keep some cash in your wallet and home for emergencies—at least enough to get your family through a long weekend.
- Make sure you have two credit cards (with available credit— ideally one with a zero balance) and two debit cards.
- Let your credit card companies know if you are travelling so they'll be less likely to freeze your cards.
- Do not show your ID with your credit card purchases or protect your key info with Wite-Out tape.
- Don't carry more than you need. Leave your passport, health care card, and SIN card at home when they are not necessary.
- Set up secure passwords and KEEP THEM SECRET.
- Do not respond to emails requesting any kind of financial information.

Chapter Three

Investments

QUICK QUIZ

1. All mutual funds are taxed the same.

True ☐

False ☐

2. To be truly diversified, you should have what percentage of your portfolio in stocks?

A. 100%

B. 50%

C. None, stocks are too risky

D. It depends on a number of factors

3. Your principal residence is considered a very safe investment.

True ☐

False ☐

4. There's absolutely no risk investing in a GIC (Guaranteed Investment Certificate) at your bank.

True ☐

False ☐

5. In Canada, you get a tax deduction on the interest you pay for your principal residence, but don't get taxed when you sell it.

True ☐

False ☐

Sort of true ☐

Investments 101

ASSET ALLOCATION

Don't put all of your eggs in one basket. I'm sure you've heard this advice before, even if you're new to investing. Or, you can follow the words of Andrew Carnegie who said, "the wise man puts all his eggs in one basket and watches the basket."

The first axiom is likely the best strategy for most novice investors. The thinking behind this strategy is that the more you diversify into different assets, the less volatility your portfolio will face.

Let me clarify a few terms before I move on.

DEFINITION CHECK

Asset allocation—Basically, investing in different assets and the percentage that you buy in relationship to your overall portfolio is the "allocation" part. So, if you were looking at investments like stocks, bonds, and cash, how much should you have of each? That depends on a number of factors that I'll cover shortly. Asset allocation refers to what assets you will buy and how much of each. An asset is any investment that is purchased with the hope that it will appreciate and gain in value from the original amount invested.

Diversification—This is an investment strategy designed to reduce exposure to risk by combining a variety of investments (real estate, stocks, and bonds) that are unlikely to all move in the same direction at the same time. Diversification reduces both the upside and the downside potential and allows for more consistent performance in a wide range of economic circumstances.

Investment portfolio—This term is used to describe all the investment you (or an institution) own, for example, stocks, bonds, or mutual funds.

Volatility—This refers to how much the value of your investments will swing up and down.

Risk—How risky is your investment? Risk could involve either the possibility that you'll lose a portion (or all) of what you invested or that your investment could be vulnerable to interest rate risk and more. (To explain interest rate risk, let's say you lock into a GIC today at 2.3% for a five-year non-redeemable GIC. You're guaranteed your principal by the bank and you have a set rate of return. However, if interest rates continue to climb over the next five years, you've risked a better interest rate by locking in.) Every single investment (no matter what any salesperson or anyone else tells you) has some type of risk attached to it—even the seemingly lowest risk investment like an old fashioned savings account.

Most financial professionals will agree that every investment portfolio needs an element of cash, debt (bonds, GICs), and equity (stocks). All of these can be purchased individually, within a mutual fund, segregated fund, or private portfolio (I'll explain all of these shortly).

The basic premise of diversification is that you'll reduce the volatility (risk in a sense too—the ups and downs) by not sticking to just one asset class (class is a type of investment segment like bonds or stocks). If you were to invest 100% of your funds into a stock mutual fund for example, you would have some diversification (you'd have at least 50 or 60 stocks in that fund, therefore buying a bunch of different eggs for your basket). But if your stock mutual fund was invested primarily in Canadian stocks and the market tanked, 100% of your investments would drop too. (Of course, if you hold on to the investment, it's just a paper loss, meaning, that the loss wouldn't be real until you tried to sell. Ideally, you would hold on to the equity mutual fund with the hope that the market will bounce back up.) If, let's say, you had 50% invested in stocks and 50% invested in bonds, these classes work very different. Mix that up even further with some stocks invested in other countries, maybe a GIC at your bank, and a few different types of bonds with different maturities and you would theoretically reduce the risk of your overall portfolio. Your investments would be diversified, hopefully the volatility (ups and downs) of your investments would be reduced and ideally, you'd have a better overall, long-term return.

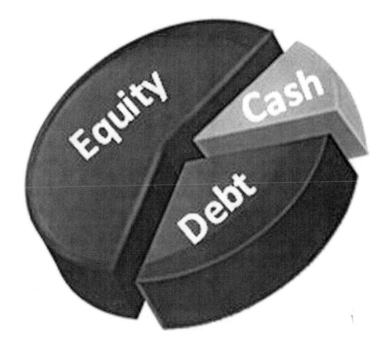

Another goal of asset allocation is to keep you invested through the ups and downs of the market and interest rate fluctuations. If you were 100% invested in the stock market and it dropped 20% in a couple of months, most investors would panic and sell (realizing their loss) even though the market might come back in a few months and finish the year off in positive territory. (Of course, you'd have to be smarter than the pros to guess the best day to get back into the market if you did sell.) It's impossible to market time (predict the high and sell and then predict the low and buy back). I assure you, no matter how confident a mutual fund manager, economist, or financial advisor is that they can time the market, they can't. If it were so, every financial expert would be overflowing with wealth and be retired on some faraway island. Instead of playing a guessing game, these financial gurus are successful because they use the many tools available to assist advisors in helping their clients pick the right balance of investments. Helping clients create the right asset mix is based on:

- The client's ability to handle risk—We all think we can handle more risk when markets are doing well, but as soon as they drop double digits, most investors change their mind and become more risk averse.
- How long they're able to stay invested—If you have only a few years before you'll retire or you need your money in the near future, you simply can't invest in a high risk or highly volatile stock, However, if you had, say, 20 years before you needed your funds, and your stomach could handle the ups and downs of the market, you could invest in something with a higher risk.
- Their level of investment knowledge—If someone is new to investing, they might want to avoid diving into riskier investments, such as stocks and equity mutual funds, until they understand and experience the movements of the market.

- Their comfort level—Even if you have 15 years before you need your money, you might not be comfortable with the moves of the market and opt for a safer bet, like a GIC or a Government of Canada bond, regardless of low rates.

I recommend that you consider the above factors before you get your feet wet, whether in the end you decide to go it alone or seek the advice of a financial professional. If you speak with a financial professional, they will take you through an investor profile including some of the aspects I outlined above. They will also consider factors, such as your age, income, gender, total wealth and assets, tax situation, feelings about the market, and more.

For calculators that will help you assess your own ideal asset allocation model, visit www.kelleykeehn.com/themoneybook.html.

What Does Asset Allocation Really Mean?

The three main categories are:
- Cash
- Debt
- Equity

CASH

Examples of Cash
- Cash in a bank account
- Term Deposit (TD) at a bank—A short-term, safe, and guaranteed investment at a bank, trust company, or credit union. Its "term" is less than a year—you could have a three- or six-month term for example. The longer the term, the higher the interest rate. The interest is higher than you'd receive on a bank account and lower than you'd receive

in a longer term investment, such as a GIC.

- Government of Canada T-bill—A short term (less than a year) government treasury purchased at a lower cost than face value but matures at face value (the spread is your profit).

Purpose of maintaining a portion of your investments in cash:

- RRIFs (which we'll cover in Chapter 5)
- Emergency savings
- For additional investment opportunities
- Prudent financial planning
- A safety net

What are the characteristics of cash investments?

- Highly liquid
- Easily accessible and without onerous fees or penalties
- Very short-term, as far as investing is concerned

Cash is a simple asset class to explain and to grasp. The debt and equity classes can be a bit more confusing. My husband is a brilliant man whom I've been with for over a decade. For fun (yes, this is a financial geek's form of fun), once in a while I'll stop him and say, "Quick, what's the difference between a stock and a bond?" He's still gets tongue-tied and has a hard time giving me a concise definition of each in just a few words.

DEBT

The debt class is also often referred to as an income class. The reason that it's called *debt* is because the investor becomes the banker. You lend your money to a bank (for a TD or GIC) or to a government or corporation for an investment and then they will owe you money similar to any other loan agreement, such as a car loan. They tell you the options for holding your money and what interest rate you'll get back in return. You might choose to have all of your interest paid when the agreement (term) is up or, in some cases such as with a GIC, you could choose to have the interest paid monthly, annually, etc. This might be a great option for a retired person needing funds to pay for their day-to-day expenses. It's also why this class is referred to as income: because the investment category has the opportunity to pay the investor income, even before the term is up.

Many of these investments that lock you in for a span of a few years also grow as a result of compound interest. Quite simply, compound interest is interest upon interest upon the original investment. Let's say you invested $100,000 and earned 3% interest paid annually. At the end of the year, you will have earned $3,000. You could take that $3,000 and spend it, or you could reinvest (or leave the interest alone) for the next year. Assuming an equal interest rate and not factoring in tax owed, you now have $103,000 to invest the next year. At the end of year two, you've earned $3,090 dollars. Add that to what you started with, and you'll round out year two with $106,090. All remaining equal again, at the end of year three, you've earned $3,182.70 and if you add that to what you started with in year three, you've ended the year with $109,272.70. At the end of year three, you earned a total of $9,272.70. If you had simply invested $100,000 a year and spent your interest (didn't reinvest it), you would have earned only $9,000. With compound interest, you earned an extra $272.70. Of course, time is a factor with compounding. The longer the investment, the more it compounds and, of course, the larger the investment and greater the rate of return, the more significant the numbers.

Debt/income examples:

- Guaranteed Investment Certificates (GICs)—These investments are purchased at a bank, credit union, or trust company. The bank guarantees that your principal (the amount invested) will be returned to you. If for any reason the bank had a problem doing so in the future, like we've seen in the United States, you're protected by CDIC (Canadian Deposit Insurance Corporation) insurance, as long as it's a major bank or trust company that falls under the protection of CDIC. GICs have terms from one to five years and can either be locked in or redeemable during the term. The latter, of course, would pay less interest as you could demand the money back from the bank whenever you wanted. With the income class, the longer you lock your funds in—that is you "lend" them out—the greater your interest will be.

- Canada Savings Bonds (CSB)—The Bank of Canada issues CSBs, which offer a competitive rate of interest and guarantee a minimum interest rate. CSBs have both regular and compound interest features and are redeemable at any time. Savings bonds work similar to GICs in the sense that you're lending your money to the government and they're paying you a rate of interest in return.

- Bonds—Bonds are complex investments with many, many options. There are books dedicated solely to explaining them. Basically, think of a bond's components as being similar to those of a GIC: there's a principal investment and then the interest or what's called a yield with a bond. You are the lender—to the Government of Canada, a province or a city—and in exchange, you're promised your original investment back. The interest you're paid on top of your principal depends on the credit worthiness of the borrower and the length of your bond. Corporations can offer bonds as well. All bonds are measured by a credit rating agency. Obviously, the worse their credit rating, the more interest they will have to pay you for investing with them. As you might suspect, the Government of Canada would pay the lowest rate of interest, as the government is safe and can simply print more money. A provincial bond would pay more than the Government of Canada, and a municipal bond (your city might need to raise money too) would pay even more than the province, as, of course, a province is more financially sound than a city.

There are three distinct differences between a bond and a GIC:

- A GIC has a shorter term than a bond. As mentioned above, a GIC offers terms from one year to five. A bond however, offers terms from ten to thirty years.

- Bonds are purchased through a bond trader and are traded on a bond market. Just because you purchased a ten-year Government of Canada bond, doesn't mean you can't sell it in year five on the bond market. That's also the main difference between a Canada Savings Bond and a Government of Canada Bond. A CSB is held in an individual's name, whereas a true bond of any type can be sold on a bond market like a stock is sold on a stock market. A GIC is generally purchased at a bank and you'll be locked in to the term and rate agreed upon by you and the bank.

- A GIC is purchased in your name (in some cases jointly with someone else) and is a strict agreement between you and the bank. A bond on the other hand can be sold on a bond market (even if you had a ten-year bond, you could sell it in year three on the open market). You can't do this with a GIC.

Bonds can be very complex investments. For the purposes of keeping this book basic, I've kept the definitions simple. If you'd like to study bonds further, try *The Bond Book* (3ʳᵈ ed) by Annette Thau.

How does the debt/income category work?

This asset class is affected by interest rates and an investor needs to be aware of "interest rate risk" (see Page 84 for a synopsis of risk). Your risk with a GIC, for example, is that if you lock in today for five years in a non-redeemable GIC at say 3.5% and interest rates for that same GIC rise to 5% in two years, you're stuck at the lower rate. However, if rates dropped, you'd benefit from receiving the higher rate until your GIC expired.

Bonds carry the same interest rate risk and a bond's value moves opposite to interest rates. If you purchased a ten-year Government of Canada bond for 5% today and interest rates start to rise, you would lose if you tried to sell your investment on a bond market. However, you'd be just fine if you held it to maturity (for the full ten years—you'd still receive the interest agreed upon).

Interest Rates   Bond Yields

Which option is better?

OPTION ONE: Ten-year Government of Canada Bond bought in 2011 with a 5% coupon. Coupon is the official name for interest when dealing with bonds. (Bonds can be stripped of their coupon— I did say bonds are complex and have different elements—but for this illustration, think of coupon as the interest rate offered.)

OPTION TWO: Ten-year Government of Canada Bond bought in 2013 with a 7% coupon.

I hope it is obvious that option two is better. As you can see, when rates rise, it's not profitable to sell a bond with a lower rate of interest. However, if the options were reversed and you purchased a bond paying 7% and interest rates dropped and the new ten-year Government of Canada bonds were now paying 5% in two years, not only did you receive interest from your bond for two years, but you could now sell it at a premium if you chose to do so (as investors out there would be willing to pay more than you did for your bond in exchange for a return that they wouldn't be able to realize at going rates).

Recap: As interest rates rise, bond values decrease and as rates drop, bond values increase. However, you can always hold on to your bond until maturity.

Why would you buy a bond?

One might buy a bond in order to add diversification to an investment portfolio and because as an asset class, bonds perform steadily and generally have less risk than an equity investment. The downside of bonds is that with the current low interest environment, your rate of return is low.

EQUITY

The equity class generally refers to stocks and investments that provide equity—another word for ownership. This is the most complex and diverse class due to the range of risk, return, and options. One can invest domestically or globally, take advantage of foreign currencies, and more.

If the three main asset classes are still a little fuzzy, I'll illustrate a few stories and provide further explanations to help clarify. Even close friends and relatives of mine that have spent many hours picking my brain about investing options and are quite well versed as investors have a difficult time describing the difference between the income/debt class and the equity/stock class.

Give it a try yourself. In one word, how would you define each class (I've omitted cash as it's simple to grasp).

EQUITY/STOCK:_____(one word answer)

INCOME/DEBT:_____(one word answer)

There are a few words that would simply define each class. I like to use "own" and "owed." With the equity class, you "own" a part of that investment. With the income class, you're "owed" money. Here's a better illustration:

Let's pretend you have a bunch of brilliant tech friends. They're on the cusp of a new project that could rival Facebook or Twitter. They know they're onto the next "it" project. However, they've just started out as a business and need cash fast. Other than CBC's *Dragon's Den*, they have three options to raise money:

1. They could borrow it from a bank. This isn't a likely option for a high-risk start-up, so, they'll have to go to the market with option two and three.

2. Their second option is to get investors to lend them money. They'll have to pay a high rate of interest for doing so if they choose this option. This is the basic premise of a bond. Going to the market and asking for a loan from the public or specific investors. In this option, they "owe" the investor money and set the time frame of the loan and enticement of the rate paid. They'd likely be considered a junk bond—a bond with a low

investment quality rating. Here's where another risk comes into play with bonds: the issuer—the entity borrowing the money. How likely are they to pay the funds back at all?

3. Their third option is to offer ownership in their company in the form of shares or equity to the investor. In this option, they'd lose some control over their company, which is why some would prefer to offer a bond. The investor shares in the ups and downs of the company. This is also the greatest risk for the investor, but it also provides the maximum opportunity for investment return.

A company can go to the market with both option two and three. A bank for example, can have bank bonds or stocks (you could purchase BMO or Scotiabank shares or, you could buy a BMO or Scotiabank bond).

Those are the three options a company wishing to seek capital has at its disposal. But what about a government? They can't go to the bank to borrow money and they can't go to the public and offer shares. The only option left is two: to offer a bond to raise money for their projects. Hence, bonds are usually thought of in relationship to a government. In our country, the Government of Canada can seek to raise funds with a bond, so can a province (for road or other work), as can a city, which would offer a municipal bond.

As mentioned before, bonds can be very complex investments. You could purchase another country's bond in a foreign currency, for example. There are bond assessment rating companies that assess the risk of each major bond and therefore, the amount of interest that each entity will pay. To sum up, the riskier the country or company, the more interest they will have to pay to entice investors. And with some bonds, investors can face a risk to their original investment.

Basic Taxation of Investments

With the cash and income/debt classes, the interest, yield, or coupon is taxed at 100%. In the equity class, when you have a profit from a sale, you are faced with what's called a capital gain, which is only taxed at 50%. When you invest in an asset and it appreciates, the selling price minus the purchase price is the capital gain. I should note that the purchase price is called the ACB—the adjusted cost base. It sounds complex but if there are fees associated with an investment that produces a capital gain, the purchase price might not actually be the ACB that the CRA (Canada Revenue Agency) uses to determine your tax payable when selling—think commissions, fees, etc.

A dividend has a more complex calculation, but basically, a stock paying a dividend (called a preferred share) means that this type of stock has more rights than a common share and the company can pay its shareholders a return of profit in a tax preferred dividend. The dividend is a return of profit from the company to the investor along with the opportunity for appreciation (or depreciation) of the stock. As definitions for preferred shares and dividends tend to be quite complex, please see my website for more information.

If you were to earn $100 of interest income, you would be taxed 100% at your marginal tax rate. If your marginal tax rate were 48%, you would pay $48 on that $100 of interest. You would pocket $52.

If you were to sell a stock and received a $100 capital gain, you would only have to pay tax on 50% or $50 in this example. If your marginal tax rate were 48%, you would pay $24 in tax. You would pocket $76.

If all things were equal (such as risk and type of investment), an investment producing capital gains, tax wise, would always be the more favourable choice. However, one should never make an investment choice based simply on tax considerations.

One note on bonds: If you were to sell your bond at a premium as discussed earlier, you would have a favourable capital gain in addition to the interest you were paid. Tax wise, think of a bond as being similar to a rental property. There are two elements to a rental property—the property itself, which may increase or decrease in value (when you sell a property other than your principal residence, you pay a capital gain if it appreciates) and the "income," which you get from your tenants, which illustrates the income a bond-holder receives. If you sell your bond at a premium, you'll have both interest income and capital gains—again, the latter is taxed more favourably.

SUMMARY OF ASSET CLASSES

Cash	Debt	Equity
• Highly liquid	• Mid- to long-term investment horizon	• Long-term investment horizon
• Generally very safe	• Lower to moderate risk	• Moderate to very high risk
• Low interest rate	• Interest rate risk	• Risk to principal (original investment is never guaranteed)
• No tax break—interest income	• Generally interest income, but if you were to sell your bond at a premium, you would have a capital gain.	• Produce capital gains when sold, which receive a 50% tax break
	• Possible risk to principal	

Advanced Asset Allocation

Asset allocation is the most basic analysis a financial advisor will perform on your investments, hopefully on a regular basis. The amount you have in stocks, bonds, and cash should be carefully considered before you invest, with decisions based on criteria such as your age, amount of time until you need your funds, ability to handle risk, and so on. The percentage split of how much you've invested in each asset depends on those factors and your mix shouldn't change unless you've had a major life change (divorce, inheritance, job loss, etc.). However, every six months to a year, certain investments will go up and down and a good advisor will sell off and purchase different assets to bring your mix back to the ideal percentage.

Advanced asset allocation factors in a few other areas in a person's life that should be viewed as a whole with their investment portfolio. There are a number of asset "classes" missing from the pie chart on Page 85, such as precious metals or art collections, but there are two major classes that you and your advisor should be paying close attention to. Can you think of what major classes are missing from the first pie chart?

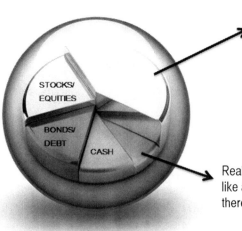

Your employment income—If you're a business owner, your company is an often forgotten asset and is a major source of one's income in a lifetime. It should be considered an asset class when assessing your overall investment portfolio.

Real estate—Because it can appreciate like a stock but the owner is paid income, there isn't a neat slot for it.

Consider the employees of the fallen company, Enron. An American energy company, before its bankruptcy in late 2001, Enron employed approximately 22,000 staff and was one of the world's leading electricity, communications, pulp and paper, and natural gas companies with "claimed" revenues of nearly $101 billion in 2000. In 2001, it was revealed that its reported revenues were sustained by accounting fraud. Enron shares dropped from over US$90 to just pennies. Because many of the employees who worked for Enron most, if not all, of their investment within the company and the industry, when Enron went down, they didn't just lose their jobs, they lost everything (stocks, pensions, etc.). Such is the case too with investing in your own industry. There's nothing wrong with it, but if you're overly invested in oil and gas, for example, and you also work in the oil and gas sector, if you face a lay-off or are getting ready to retire, your investments will likely suffer at the same time.

Many individuals don't really understand the importance of the nuances of their investing personalities, nor do some advisors. Think about the risky entrepreneur. They're likely the same individuals who will be attracted to risky investments. They likely don't have a pension plan and most of their investments will usually be tied up in their businesses. When they invest, they should choose a lower risk, complementary asset classes to offset their already high-risk business. Here's the opposite scenario: a professor with tenure. He has excellent job security, likely a great pension, employee benefits, and more. Viewing his employment, it's fairly low risk. His tendency for investing is also likely low risk, when he actually could use the risk to balance out his portfolio.

NEGATIVE CORRELATION

Sounds like a complex notion, but it's actually quite simple and so essential to achieving the most effective rate on your portfolio with the least amount of risk possible.

Imagine that you arrived at a resort town. You have two possible investment options: buy into a company that sells umbrellas (banking on how many rainy days will occur), or one that sells suntan lotion (banking on how many sunny days the year will produce).

Generally when it's raining it isn't sunny and vice versa. So the correct bet would be, a little of both. That's the essential idea with negative correlation—you want investments that don't correlate to each other because if they do, your entire portfolio is either going to go up or down. You need investments that are vastly different to reduce your risk and maximize potential return. The old adage of not putting all your eggs in one basket is indeed sage advice—just make sure you don't have a bunch of baskets with the same eggs in them.

There's one additional option in that resort town and that's the local hot dog stand. It doesn't turn a huge profit for the owner or investors, however, come rain or shine, it still turns a consistent profit. Allocating some of your investments to cash (or the food stand) is prudent and you want to ensure that you have the right mix of bonds and stocks and a variety of each so you're not fully out of luck if it rains or shines most of the year (so to speak).

Mutual Funds

QUICK QUIZ

1. Are mutual funds a good investment?
2. Are mutual funds safe or risky?
3. How many mutual funds are on the Canadian market?

First, I truly believe that there is generally no good or bad investment, but only what's good or bad for you. There's a plethora of investing choices out there and other than the obviously fraudulent options, it really depends on where you are in life, your comfort zones, the amount of time you want to spend managing your money, and the amount of money you have to invest. Mutual funds can be a great vehicle for some and far too expensive for others, such as those with a large portfolio, for example.

As to how risky or safe they are, at the time of printing, fundlibrary.com reported that there were over 9,500 mutual funds in Canada, while funddata.com keeps track of 16,000 mutual fund and investment related products. With that range and selection, there is a range of mutual funds from the super safe, right up to the extremely risky and everything in between.

WHAT IS A MUTUAL FUND?

A mutual fund is simply a pooling of assets that a fund company manages on your behalf. You can, for example, buy all sorts of cash assets, bonds, or stocks on your own or purchase them within a mutual fund for a number of benefits that I'll explain shortly.

To illustrate, you can purchase each asset class on its own, however, for some investments, the minimum is quite high.

To purchase a T-Bill, for example, you would need $100,000 to buy this short-term investment (T stands for treasury).

You would need to buy a number of bonds with different maturity dates to have a properly diversified bond portfolio. This diversity can easily be achieved in a bond mutual fund for an investor with a modest amount of money to invest.

To be diversified with a modest portfolio, it would be challenging to do so through buying individual stocks. For example, if you had $10,000 to invest, depending on the stocks you were looking at and their price, you would be able to purchase a set number, and chances are, the number of stocks would be low. However, if you purchased an equity mutual fund, you would have exposure to 40-60 stocks or more— certainly, a greater diversification than outside a mutual fund.

Or, you can purchase pretty much any asset within a mutual fund or any combination thereof, since there is such a wide selection of funds on the market. You can have a cash-only type of fund called a money market fund (very low risk mix of short-term investments with low current returns), you could have a bond fund with all types of bonds expiring at different dates and paying different yields, or you could have an equity fund investing in pretty much any country in the world, which could include dozens of stocks. There are many specialty funds on the market, such as precious metals funds, real estate funds, funds focused on the baby boomer market, and much more.

You can purchase any of these assets
individually or just about any combination
within a mutual fund.

WHY WOULD YOU INVEST IN A MUTUAL FUND?

Regular Investing	Within a Mutual Fund
• Ultimate control over which investments are purchased (i.e., you want to buy particular stocks or bonds yourself)	• Have a wide range of investment options that are pooled
• Need to monitor your investments yourself or hire a broker to buy and sell on your behalf	• The mutual fund manager buys and sells on your behalf
• Stocks, for example, can only be sold or bought if there is a buyer and seller for the stock that you'd like to buy or sell.	• Can buy or sell your units (mutual funds don't offer shares per se—instead you purchase units that rise and fall) any business day.
• Ideal for investors with larger portfolios and/or for individuals who will watch their investments closely.	• Ideal for investors with modest amounts to invest. For a minimum investment of say $500 in an equity mutual fund an investor might have exposure to dozens of stocks. Without the mutual fund option, $500 might not purchase even a modest number of shares in one stock. Diversification is absolutely a benefit for the small investor. Plus, you can have a monthly purchase plan with a mutual fund (most funds start at $25 a month), which you can't with individual securities.

WHAT ARE THE BENEFITS OF A MUTUAL FUND?

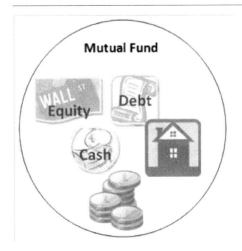

• Professional money managers are buying and selling investments on your behalf
• Maximum diversification for smaller portfolios
• Ease of investing monthly and in small initial investments
• Thousands of mutual funds to choose from

Consider that on October 27, 2010, one share of Berkshire Hathaway (Warren Buffet's company) was trading at over $122,000. An investor would have needed a sizable portfolio to take advantage of Mr. Buffet's investment acumen without putting all their eggs in one basket (even if you had a million dollars to invest, purchasing one stock of Berkshire Hathaway would represent over 10% of your holdings). In a mutual fund, for a minimum investment of $500, you can buy a piece of Buffet's company if the fund has it in its holdings.

Let's assume that you'd like to purchase gold. For many reasons, it's inconvenient to buy bullion, stash it in a safe in your home, or lock it away in a safety deposit box. You might then think that purchasing gold stocks would be simpler than owning the physical pieces of metal, but would this give you the diversity that you'd like? A third option exists, especially if you're not sure if gold, silver, or other metals individually might give the best bang for your buck. Within a precious metals mutual fund, the manager buys and sells the metals that she believes will perform the best. You have maximum diversification with one single purchase.

WHO IS A MUTUAL FUND RIGHT FOR AND WHO IS IT NOT?

Mutual funds are perfect for investors looking for:

* Maximum diversification with a modest investment amount;
* The option to invest monthly;
* Don't want to spend much time buying, selling, and monitoring investments;
* The ability to purchase on behalf of others, like parents and grandparents purchasing RESPs for children/grandchildren.

When does a mutual fund not make sense? It generally comes down to fees. I'll explain the fees shortly. At a certain portfolio dollar amount, mutual funds become too expensive because of the high management fees and even if an investor doesn't want to actively be involved in the buying and selling of assets in their portfolio, private portfolio management at a bank, brokerage, or trust company usually makes the most financial sense. For example, if the average fee for a balanced mutual fund portfolio is 2.75%, a private banking portfolio might charge under 1% (it all depends on the amount of the assets). The problem for the average Canadian is that most private banking services are only offered to investors with at least $500,000 of assets. So, for most Canadians, mutual funds make solid sense.

But if you'd prefer to monitor and trade your own investments yourself, regardless of the size of your portfolio, mutual funds might not be right for you.

WHERE DO YOU BUY MUTUAL FUNDS AND HOW?

You can purchase mutual funds through a financial advisor, mutual fund salesperson at a bank or brokerage, or within your self-directed account.

WHAT ARE THE FEES?

The greatest criticism against mutual funds in Canada is their high management fees compared to other countries.

Generally, it's not considered good manners to ask people how much money they make. But, with a new study out that criticizes Canada's mutual funds for the high fees they charge, that's a rule you might want to start breaking, at least when it comes to dealing with investment advisors and the products they sell.

A study came out from Morningstar USA, a leading independent investment research firm that's widely considered the authority on mutual fund performance. In this study, Morningstar looked at funds in 16 countries, and the bad news is, when it comes to mutual fund fees, Canada failed because of the level of our MERs—Management Expense Ratios. These are fees that cover everything from the salary of the fund manager to compensation for the investment advisors, like yours perhaps, who buy these funds for their clients.

Oddly enough, the report didn't cite specific numbers or averages so I did a little research myself. Depending on the year, I found the average Canadian equity fund has an MER of 2.25% compared to 1.42% for the average American fund.

Now the report does admit that in many countries some costs are not bundled exactly the way they are in Canada, so that may account for some of the differences between Canadian funds and others around the world. And in fairness, our mutual fund industry was rated a B- due to the safe regulations in place. But even taking all that into consideration, it still seems that the fees here are higher than elsewhere in the world.

Why should you care about the fees your fund is charging?

The idea of investment in mutual funds is that they take a lot of the worry away that can be associated with investing. Why spend your time and energy trying to pick individual stocks or bonds when you can hand the job over to a professional fund manager? Plus, over 90% of Canadians who invest, own mutual funds.

But here's why these fees matter. When you look at rates of return for mutual funds, you have to remember that they are calculated after the management expense fees are taken off. So the fee represents money that's going to the mutual fund company and possibly to your investment advisor.

Let's look at how much just 1% can affect your investments over time:

- Assuming a $100,000 investment
- Invested for 20 years
- Not factoring in inflation
- No further investments added
- All investment types remain constant in both examples
- Rates and MERs remain constant in both examples of 20 years

Scenario 1

Rate of return for XYZ mutual fund is 6.25% before fees. The MER (management fee of this fund) is 2.25% and so your net rate of return is 4%. At the end of 20 years, your investment would be worth $219,112.31.

Scenario 2

You're able to find a very similar mutual fund, index fund, or ETF that charges just 1% less in fees. You invest the same amount and actually earn the same 6.25% return. However, because the MER is now just 1.25%, your net return is 5%. At the end of 20 years, this investment would be worth $265,329.77.

Of course, if the amount invested was larger and you had a longer time frame for investing, the fee difference would be even more substantial. In this example, with the exact same rate of return, but a fee difference of just 1%, Scenario 2 would have earned $46,217.46 more than Scenario 1. Obviously 1% is enough to take notice of and for you to pay equal attention to when examining the fees in your own investments (or, take your advisor to task and get all fees, hidden and otherwise, in writing).

I'm not suggesting for a moment that your financial professional should work for free: Everybody deserves fair compensation. The investor, however, should be aware of what those fees are and what their advisor is providing in exchange for advice and planning services.

What concerns me is that a recent Angus Reid poll found that of the people who have money invested in mutual funds more than 50% had "no idea" what they were being charged. The industry shouldn't be satisfied with that; they should want their customers to be well informed.

So if MERs and investment fees are new to you or you think you need a refresher, here are three questions to ask your financial professional:

1. What exactly am I invested in and why?
2. What fees am I paying with my investments? And an even better qualifying question would be: If I cashed out everything tomorrow, what fees, if any, would I have to pay?
3. What biases to you have?

Every advisor has a bias and is limited by the licences that they hold. Ask your advisor what his or hers are. If they aren't licensed to sell stocks and bonds (only mutual funds for example), chances are they aren't going to recommend stocks and bonds to you.

Don't be afraid to shop around and get a second opinion if you don't get the answers you're seeking. You have a right to know, so start by simply digging out your most recent investment statement and calling your advisor today.

Another slam against the mutual fund industry is that most managers rarely outperform the index (which I explain in the coming pages). Essentially, an actively managed mutual fund has a manager making decisions about which securities to buy and sell in a given day, and this oversight is used to justify the higher fee. When you purchase an index fund or an ETF, these investments are simply mirroring the indexes and thus, since there's no active management, the fees are considerably lower. With an index fund or ETF, as the index increases or decreases, so does your investment. The appeal of mutual funds with active management is that the manager can hopefully mitigate losses in a down turn. The big criticism of mutual funds is that they don't seem to be able to beat the market averages overall (some do, but it's a small percentage of the mutual fund market).

DEFINITION CHECK

Index funds are mutual funds that seek to mirror the returns of a market index by investing  directly in the securities that make up that index. These funds are passively managed and tend to have lower fees than actively managed funds.

Segregated funds are funds with a recurring payment offered by an insurance company, which guarantees a specific return on the investment upon maturity. It is similar to a mutual fund but the funds are kept separate from the issuing company's other investment funds. Segregated funds also contain other benefits such as the exemption from certain fees, for example the probate fee that would normally be charged when the fund is passed to a beneficiary. Seg funds, as they're also called, can be a good investment under very specific circumstances. However, because their MERs or fees are even higher than those of mutual funds, many critics wonder if the extra cost is worth any of the guarantees (which have been reduced in recent years).

For example, the sales pitch for some segregated funds is that if you hold your fund for at least ten years (in many cases) you'll get a guaranteed return of all of your principal investment (although in many cases today, the offer has been reduced to 75% back of your original investment). If in ten years all you got back was what you invested or ¾ of it, most would agree that that's likely not the best investment. Plus, the higher MERs will erode any of your profits if the markets perform during the time you're invested.

For definitions of ETFs, and other complex investment terms, please visit my website at www.kelleykeehn.com/themoneybook. html.

WHAT ARE THE **NASDAQ**, DOW JONES, AND **TSX?**

We often hear radio reports during the drive home from work or on the evening news about point gain or loss of these indices. I've included below a few simple definitions to help you understand their relevance and what they mean. I should note that the word *indices* is simply a finance term to describe many indexes.

The stock exchanges

An exchange is really just that: It's a financial medium for investors to buy and sell their investments with intermediaries, offering some consumer protection, such as securities commissions and requirements for prospectuses to be filed.

Each exchange will have thousands of stocks represented and available for buying and selling. The TSX 300, for example, is not necessarily the 300 best stocks on the Canadian exchange but the 300 most actively traded. When an index is up or down by a certain number of percentage points, it's a fair but vague indication of how that country or sector of stocks is performing.

- *TSX 300*—This index represents the trends of the Toronto Stock Exchange by tracking the prices of the 300 most actively traded and influential stocks.
- *TSX*—This is Canada's largest stock exchange (previously known as the TSE) and is headquartered in Toronto, the third largest financial centre in North America. The TSE was changed to the current TSX because "TSE" is used by the Tokyo Stock Exchange.
- *The NASDAQ*—This index is the largest electronic screen-based equity securities market in the US, with approximately 3,200 companies being traded.
- *The S&P 500*—This index contains the stocks of 500 leading US corporations and is managed by Standard and Poor's. After the Dow Jones Industrial Average, the S&P is the most widely watched index of large cap US stocks.

WHAT IS A RECESSION?

A recession is a time of economic downturn, constriction, and the temporary decline of stock markets and the economy as a whole. It generally starts with climbing inflation. As the markets heat up, things start to cost more. Employees expect higher wages to keep up with the higher costs. Corporations' earnings must grow to satisfy investors who are always willing to sell their interests.

When interest rates are low and the economy is strong, people as a whole feel confident about the future. Low interest rates allow them to purchase homes, cars, and other goods at reasonable rates. As inflation rises due to demand, the federal government steps in to increase rates so we don't see a repeat of double-digit interest rates like we did in the '80s. If you remember that time in Canada, many homeowners were walking away from their real-estate holdings, handing the mortgage and obligation over to the bank or lender. Rates became so high and unmanageable that many people couldn't make their payments.

In today's environment, the federal government will try to stave off out-of-control inflation by raising rates slowly. In doing so, they intend to stabilize the economy before it gets out of hand. The hope is that if interest rates go up, consumers will spend less and demand fewer goods and the economy will then stabilize itself. It's sort of like pruning your trees. It's necessary to trim back the growth at times for a more robust tree in the future.

Certain other factors outside of interest rates can contribute to not just a recession, but a total collapse or depression, such as the global one in 2008 that much of the world is still recovering from today. Although the effects of this financial crisis were felt in Canada, the US was much harder hit. The burst of the US housing bubble in late 2008 is still forcing many homeowners to walk away from their houses.

There are many factors and economic indicators that may cause a downturn in the economy, including war, catastrophes, unemployment, and more. Basically, when a society feels poor due to low demand for products and services, the high cost to purchase cars and homes on credit, and a low feeling of job security, this has a ripple effect on the country as a whole. The opposite is true when markets are swinging upwards and interest rates and inflation are still low.

WHAT ARE BULLS AND BEARS?

Bulls and bears are used to represent the up and downs of the stock market or how an expert feels about a particular stock.

A bull market is on the upswing. When financial professionals feel bullish about a stock or the economy, they believe a positive move forward is imminent and would suggest buying.

A bear market is moving downwards. Financial professionals

feel bearish about a stock when they believe it's ready to tank. In this case, they would suggest selling.

Real Estate

I hope you now have a solid grasp of the investment options in Canada along with a basic understanding of how markets function. However, there's one asset you're likely quite familiar with, the largest non-investment you'll ever own—your home.

It's generally accepted in the financial world that one's home is not an investment. If you're a homeowner, however, you'd likely disagree. The thought behind this notion is, as far as your retirement plan is concerned, that if you won't sell an asset entirely to fund your retirement, it's not an investment. However, it certainly is an asset and one not to be ignored no matter your future intent with it. You'll see in a later case study that in some cases the equity in your home can be used to your advantage, or to your detriment if not managed prudently.

In Canada, when you sell your principal residence (you must live in a property for at least six months for it to be considered a principal residence), you don't pay tax on any of the growth. If you purchased your home for $300,000, for example, and by the time you sold for $500,000 20 years later, you'd get to pocket $200,000 tax-free or roll it into a new purchase of some type. Because you don't pay tax on the increase in your home's value, you do not get a tax break on the interest that you pay on your mortgage. This Canadian model is the opposite of the US. Perhaps this is why our friends to the south take out bigger mortgages and don't focus on paying them off as quickly as Canadians; they get a tax break on the interest on the mortgage of their principal residence. However, Americans do pay tax when they sell their home for a gain.

If you decided to turn your basement into a rental suite or call a portion of your home an "office" with the sincere intent of earning a profit, you will be able to write off a portion of your mortgage and other housing expenses, like rent. However, be sure it isn't just a hobby that you're calling a business. The Canada Revenue Agency (CRA), our government tax collection agency, has become very cognizant of those claiming to be generating income just to write off a portion of their housing expenses.

REAL ESTATE AS AN INVESTMENT

If you have a piece of real estate that isn't your principal residence (another house, condo, building, etc.), when you sell that property, you will pay tax on the gain or be able to use the loss (if you sold at a loss) against other income. I won't get into the tax technicalities, but in this example, if you used borrowed funds for your real estate investment, you would get a tax deduction on the interest you paid (similarly to other investments as well).

Q: *When Jaylen's grandmother passed away, Jaylen was left a rental property with no mortgage. A recent appraisal told her it was worth about $300,000. Her own house, she suspects, is worth about $450,000 and she has a mortgage of $225,000. What should Jaylen do, if anything?*

A: I hope you came up with juggling her mortgage around on the properties as the answer. Why? The mortgage on her home is not tax deductible. Since she rents out the property that her grandmother bequeathed to her, she's earning income from it. If she moved all or most of her current mortgage to her rental property (at renewal so she doesn't pay a penalty), that interest she's paying would now be used to offset the income she's receiving from her renters.

Because your home is still likely your largest asset, even if it's not technically considered an investment, you should certainly pay attention to its value. We'll examine some strategies for getting your mortgage paid down sooner to increase that asset in Chapter 6.

Recap

- Spread the wealth and diversify your portfolio. Remember not to put all your eggs in one basket. But also make sure that you don't have a bunch of baskets with the same eggs in them!
- A well-balanced portfolio should have cash, debt, and equity.
- Cash is important as a safety net to allow for future investment opportunities, and as an emergency fund that is easily accessible.
- Debt refers to a product where you (the investor) become the lender.
- Equity refers to the investments that increase in value generating a profit and means that you have "ownership."
- There are number of exceptional financial professionals to help you reach your goals, however, before seeking external advice, do your own basic research. Also, don't be afraid to shop around. Please visit www.kelleykeehn.com/themoneybook. html for a list of resources to assist you in finding the right financial advisor in your area.

Congratulations for making it through this chapter! Investment basics aren't really that basic. If you still have questions or would like to learn more about any of the investments outlined in this chapter, please head to my site for resources that will take you to the next level of investment learning.

An Interview with Rob Carrick

I checked in with Rob Carrick, a *Globe and Mail* columnist and author of *Rob Carrick's Guide to What's Good, Bad and Downright Awful in Canadian Investments Today*, for his top three financial tips for Canadians.

His first tip was to stop using debt to finance purchases. It sounds so simple, but people just aren't thinking this out. Rob noted that with many credit cards charging rates of 19%, he feels that most people just don't think about the costs and consequences: they simply spend beyond their means. Ignoring these considerations can cost many years of payments and far too much paid in interest. He notes that if more consumers thought out their purchases and either held off on making the purchase, waited to save up for it, or used lower interest debt options, such as a loan or line of credit, that they would ultimately be in a better place.

His second tip was about the fees paid for investing; not only the fees paid for the actual investment (MERs with mutual funds and commissions), but also the fees paid to your investment advisor. Rob suggests that a good acid test to determine if your advisor is worth the fees would be if he or she offers solid financial, retirement, tax and estate planning (and more). If they're simply selling you an investment without the advice, you should look around and ensure you're getting your dollar's worth.

Lastly, Rob hoped that this year (it's as good as any), Canadians would stop adding to their credit card debt and start chipping away at it. Prudent and simple, yet we're in more debt than we've ever been. According to the Credit Counselling Society (reported in the *Edmonton Journal* January 25, 2011), the average household debt is at nosebleed levels—it reached 148% of annual disposable income in the third quarter of 2010—and with interest rates likely to rise later this year, many consumers are flirting with disaster. So,

Canadians obviously aren't heeding the common sense and prudent advice Rob Carrick is providing.

Chapter 4

Avoiding Investment Schemes

Quick Quiz

1. A guaranteed return of 10% is reasonable to expect.

True   ☐

False   ☐

2. Research of an investment is the responsibility of:

A. Your financial advisor

B. The person recommending the investment

C. Government agencies

D. You

3. If you've been with your financial advisor for five years or more, you don't need to check up on their credentials.

True   ☐

False   ☐

4. You should always request investment specifics in writing, even from those you know and trust.

True   ☐

False   ☐

5. If an investment has a short window of time to get in, you should:

A. Invest immediately

B. Get a second opinion

C. Check the person out with provincial and federal agencies and professional organizations

D. Run

Spotting the Crooks

2009 was a wild year with a media frenzy over the antics of Ponzi scheme artists Bernie Madoff in the US and Earl Jones in Canada. If you didn't read or watch the sensational stories break, Madoff was part of the largest Ponzi scheme in history, defrauding thousands of investors of billions of dollars. He was arrested in December 2008. Around July 2009, Canadian Ponzi schemer Earl Jones' clients' cheques started bouncing. Then the house of cards started to tumble. Jones swindled around 158 customers out of an estimated $50 to $100 million and was labelled the Canadian Bernie Madoff.

At the height of the media attention, the number one question I was asked (almost on a daily basis) was, would I, a former financial professional for over a decade and financial consumer advocate for the past six years, have been able to spot Madoff and Jones as the shysters they were? I've thought a great deal about that question and always have the same response.

Before I answer, let's look at the lure of both of these nefarious men. Both were reportedly charming, fun, generous, and someone you'd trust your money with. Madoff made his investments even more appealing by making them "exclusive." It was reported that you couldn't just invest with him; you had to be invited. When investors received the call that he had an opening for them to invest their money, rarely would anyone say no. Madoff too had the credentials that even the most expert of financial professional wouldn't question. (Although, throughout the years many did question his numbers, their concerns fell on deaf ears.) As a stockbroker, investment advisor, and non-executive chairman of the NASDAQ stock market, this guy was *the* investment guru. You don't question or interview gurus; you brag when they invite you into their club.

Reports of Jones were similar. He was a gregarious, fun-loving fellow who had an equally tight group of investors from his church and social circle. He was trusted. After all, if you had several friends and family members with Jones, why bother to do the due diligence to find out his credentials, right?

To answer the question so often asked of me around that time, first, I'll look at Madoff. Even with all that I know about how investments work, no, I don't think I would have resisted the lure to invest with Madoff had I been invited (and lived in NYC and been part of his exclusive group). Based on his level of expertise and the fact that much smarter experts than I, such as hedge fund managers, trusted the guy, I admit, I likely wouldn't have done the due diligence to ensure that he was legit (if it was even possible given how secretive his reporting was). Also consider that the evil genius behind Madoff's longevity was his reasonable rate of return. That word reasonable is debatable; however, it wasn't a red flag—at first, anyway. Over many years, Madoff's investors consistently received a rate of return around 10% per year and not a bells and whistles 14% or 18%. His 10% returns could fly just under the radar. However, those individuals who did attempt to shut him down over the years tried to prove that there was no way to consistently provide that return. For the average investor, though, those returns don't seem like a number to raise concern about (although, it still should have when you consider that guaranteed investments would have only returned low to mid one-digit returns). In the case of Madoff, even in theoretical hindsight, I'm pretty sure I too would have been duped.

But looking back at Earl Jones, I'm quite confident that I would have been able to spot him and his fraudulent operation, and frankly, I can't believe that no one blew the whistle on him sooner. How can I be so sure? The first question I would have asked Jones would have been, "What licences do you hold?" And, the answer would be none. Actually, he wasn't licensed to sell any financial products. I'm sure he would have tried to talk his way out of admitting his lack of licences, likely by making some vague reference to his experience and then he would have artfully wrapped the conversation back to something comfortable. After all, Jones had become close friends with his clients; many possibly considered him family. And if you have dealt with someone for many years, how do you one day start asking questions? But just a few phone calls to the Mutual Fund Dealers Association (MFDA), the Investment Industry Regulatory Organization of Canada (IIROC), or a provincial/territorial securities commission would have saved so many people a great deal of financial heartache.

Sure there has to be some level of trust between financial professionals and their clients, but blind trust is a dangerous thing. When I was in the investment industry, I had countless clients who, after I presented them with several detailed investment options, would simply tell me, "Oh, you decide for us—we trust you implicitly." There is no one you should trust that deeply when it comes to your money. And you need to empower and protect yourself to know the warning signs and what questions you need to ask before handing over your hard-earned money or signing on any dotted line.

The RCMP is overwhelmed with cases of fraud of all types. In my discussions with the Alberta Securities Commission I learned that preemptive strategies are your greatest allies. Trying to recoup lost funds from schemes is nearly hopeless. But, you can arm yourself with a solid understanding of what to do before a tempting, too-good-to-be-true offer is placed in your lap or recommended by a trusted friend or family member. When it came to Jones, so many wondered why he wasn't caught sooner. How could he continue to call himself a financial advisor, take clients' funds, and not even be licensed? Remember this—*anyone can hang out their sign calling themselves a financial advisor/planner or offer an investment.* If they're not licensed with a governing financial body or organization, it's impossible for them to be monitored. If just a few of Jones' clients had questioned his qualifications and called around, he certainly would have been discovered by authorities sooner.

SCAM SENSOR AND RED FLAGS: QUESTIONS TO ASK YOURSELF AND THE SELLER:

1. Does this investment offer:
   a. High returns with low risk
   b. A tax-free offshore investment opportunity
   c. An opportunity usually only available to the wealthy or industry insiders
   d. You're not sure what it offers

2. You want to invest because:
   a. Your friends or family made money from the investment and think you can too
   b. It sounds like a good deal and you don't want to miss out
   c. You can make enough money from this investment to do what you really want (e.g., retire well, give more to charity, help your family)
   d. You're not sure why you want to invest

3. The person who is selling you the investment is:
   a. Registered to sell investments
   b. A family member, a friend, or a member of a church or club that you belong to
   c. A person you recently met
   d. You're not sure who is selling the investment

We'd all like to find a great investment that guarantees financial security, but unfortunately some offers are just too good to be true.

If an investment you're interested in sounds like any of the ones below, STOP! The investment might be a scam.

Take a look at some red flags that could signal that an investment opportunity is too good to be true.

"Guaranteed high returns—no risk!"

"Insider tips—profit like the experts!"

"Offshore investment—tax free!"

"Don't miss this opportunity—get in now!"

"Great investment opportunity—your friends can't be wrong!"

Are you wondering if the investment you're interested in is legit? Did you know that 42% of Albertans alone believe they have been approached with a possible fraudulent investment? In fact, 12% of Albertans who had previously been approached with a possible fraudulent investment eventually became victims. And nationally, based on the Canadian Securities Administrators (CSA) Investor Index 2009, 38% of Canadians have been approached with a fraudulent investment and 11% actually invested money in what turned out to be a fraudulent investment. It can happen to you. Check first and learn to ask the right questions before you invest.

See the end of this chapter for further resources on how to protect your money and avoid investment mistakes. Be sure to visit your provinces' securities commission and the Canadian Securities Administrators' websites for those on the disciplinary watch list and more. Please also visit www.kelleykeehn.com/themoneybook. html for a complete and up-to-date list of resources (as websites change so frequently).

The following are definitions of some of the major investment schemes out there. It's important to know about these schemes; knowing how they work is one of the best ways to protect your hard-earned money.

DEFINITION CHECK

Ponzi Schemes—A Ponzi scheme promises high rates of return with little or no risk to investors. Unbeknownst to the investors, however, returns are paid from their own money or money paid by new investors rather than from profit. There is no legitimate investment. This scheme will usually pay promised returns to early investors, as long as new investing occurs. Existing investors are often promised extraordinary returns and commissions for bringing in new investors. These schemes usually collapse on themselves as new investments stop and investors lose some or all of their money.

Pyramid Schemes—In a pyramid scheme, participants actively promote the scheme and try to make money solely by recruiting new participants into the program. Participants move up the "pyramid" as new investors buy in. However, when new participants cease to exist, the scheme collapses. Pyramid schemes are often advertised as Gifting or Networking Clubs. Promoters of pyramid schemes refer to "Gifting" and claim that it is legal. If participants enter into a scheme with the expectation of profit—this not a gift exchange. A gift is something that does not involve the receipt of a benefit. Typically, the majority of those who invest in pyramid schemes lose their investment and can become the subject of investigations by the police and Canada Revenue Agency.

Investors approached about an investment with these characteristics should make sure to do their research before investing. Do a background check on the individuals or company offering the investment opportunity.

Pump and Dump—Pump and Dump is an investment scheme where fraudsters heavily promote or "pump" the purchase of specific company stock, which creates high demand and drives up the prices of the stock. The individuals behind the promotion then sell or "dump" their shares at the increased price and stop promoting the stock, which leaves other investors with stock that is worth far less than what they initially paid for the stock.

Unscrupulous promoters or brokers will often hype a stock through the use of company websites, online bulletin boards, chat rooms, and online investment newsletters. They may even go so far as to create false press releases or mislead investors with claims of a revolutionary product approved by a federal government agency. After the price skyrockets, the promoter or broker sells the stock to an unsuspecting investor and pockets the large profit.

Scam Marketing

Some people who use paid advertisements to promote their investment opportunities may not be properly registered to trade in securities. As well, certain ads may provide misleading information to the public regarding potential investments. These ads can appear in newspapers, magazines, television, radio, newsletters, online, or on billboards.

In many cases, investments described in the advertisements may look or sound legitimate, but unless investors verify this first with an objective source, such as their provincial or territorial securities regulator, they could risk committing their money to a misleading or illegitimate opportunity. In this situation, once money changes hands, it's often difficult or impossible for investors to get their money back.

Regardless of the source, investors should protect themselves by researching every investment opportunity before investing. While no investment is without risk, investors can research opportunities to lessen the risk of falling victim to a scheme. Investors shouldn't assume an opportunity is legitimate based on where it appears or how it is presented.

Investment Clubs

Investment clubs generally consist of a group of people who share a common interest in investing. They may or may not pool their resources together. While they give you a new way to meet others and learn more about investing, it is wise to keep a few things in mind.

Participating in a group such as an investment club can give you a feeling of camaraderie, but can also lead to a false sense of security. People often believe that others have done their homework regarding an investment and therefore they can trust their judgment and don't feel they also have to do their own research. And, in a close-knit group, some investors might be less willing to ask questions, as they don't want to appear uninformed in front of their peers.

In addition, there might be others in your investment club who have different financial goals than you or might be comfortable with a higher level of risk than you. Never feel pressured to invest in something that isn't right for you.

Finally, some promoters of investment opportunities will tell you that you need to be a member of their club before you can invest in their product. Be wary of this type of condition, as there may be hidden fees that you aren't aware of.

Real Estate Investment Opportunities

As with any investment, if you are approached about an investment opportunity in real estate securities, it is important to look carefully at what exactly you are being offered. An unsuitable investment can have a damaging financial impact on you and your family.

WHEN IS A REAL ESTATE TRANSACTION A SECURITY?

Be sure to understand your real estate investment opportunity. For example, is the offering a security?

If the sale involves a scheme or arrangement whereby the purchaser may earn a return through the efforts of a third party in connection with the real estate, it may be considered to be the sale of a security.

In other words, if a buyer purchases a piece of real estate for a set price to take ownership on a set date, that is likely a real estate transaction. If the seller retains ownership of the property and a buyer purchases an interest in the property or its owner, expects a return on his or her investment, and neither plays a role in the management of it nor occupies the property as tenant, then the transaction may be the sale of a security.

If a sale of security occurs it will be subject to the requirements of the securities laws applicable in your jurisdiction, and as such must be conducted by or through a registrant, under a prospectus, or by way of an exemption from the prospectus requirements.

COMMONLY USED PROMOTION TACTICS

It is common for real estate investment companies to advertise in order to spark your interest in their opportunity. Here are some ways you might be introduced to the investment opportunity:

- Professional looking websites, emails, advertisements, flyers, and/or invitation in the mail
- Radio ads or tradeshow sales pitches that appeal to your lifestyle goals
- Paid real estate advertorials (advertisements designed to look like regular news articles)
- Invitations to seminars with free perks, such as a free dinner or travel. Read more about real estate investment seminars below.
- Word of mouth appeals through friends, family, or co-workers who are interested, have already invested in the company, or may have something to gain in recruiting you.

REAL ESTATE INVESTMENT SEMINARS

Anytime you are approached about a real estate investment opportunity, it is important to look carefully at what exactly the opportunity is offering. Making an unsuitable investment can have a social and financial impact on you and your family.

What are real estate investment seminars?

- Real estate investment companies may invite potential investors to a "seminar" through an ad in a newspaper or magazine, a phone call, an email or post letter invitation, a booth at a trade show, or word of mouth from family, friends, or co-workers.
- The seminar may include a motivational speaker, an investment expert, or even a self-made millionaire who may give advice on investing and will explain how investors can get involved.
- Some of these real estate investment opportunities make their money by charging seminar attendance fees, selling high-priced reports or books, and selling property and investments through high-pressure sales tactics.
- Real estate investment companies holding the seminars may suggest following high-risk investment strategies, such as bor-

rowing huge sums of money to buy into the investment or promoting investments that involve lending or borrowing money on unsuitable terms.

- The companies may offer to fly investors to the property location to view the real estate development. This tactic could be used to pressure an investor to commit to a deal without giving them time to obtain independent information or advice. Investors sometimes end up having to pay for their travel and accommodation if no investment is made.

CHECK FIRST

Protect yourself by learning to ask the right questions. Do not let anyone pressure you into making decisions about money or investments without getting independent financial advice.

- Before attending an investment seminar, conduct your own research. If, after doing so, you believe the seminar might be worthwhile, seek independent professional investment advice before deciding to attend.
- Remember that family members and friends may try to involve you in an opportunity without understanding the level of investment risk. Again, you should seek independent advice (from a lawyer or registered financial advisor).
- Check with your provincial securities commission and real estate council to see any action has been taken against the promoters or their companies. Remember that even if these governing bodies have not taken any action to date, this does not mean the opportunity is suitable for your risk level.
- If you have questions about the tax implications of the investment, contact Canada Revenue Agency (www.cra-arc.gc.ca).
- Be cautious about committing to any investment at a seminar— the atmosphere at these events can be quite charged and

exciting. You should only make investment decisions after you have taken some time to think about them, conducted your own independent research, and, most importantly, sought advice from an independent financial advisor.

Spot the "Red Flags" of an Unsafe Securities Investment

If you hear some of these commonly used sales pitches, take some time to think about whether the securities investment opportunity is right for you:

- Above average returns with little or no risk. No investment is risk free and, generally, the higher the return, the higher the risk—consider what you are willing to lose.
- Offers of loans or suggestions of ways to finance the investment (e.g., remortgaging your house) and further investment seminars.
- Claims of a secret or exclusive technique for building wealth.
- Limited time offer that discourages investors from getting independent advice.
- Promises to "be a millionaire in three years," "get rich quick," or "have the retirement you have always dreamed of."
- High membership fees with vague explanation of forms you must sign.
- Talk of tax avoidance, moving money offshore, or using RRSP eligibility as a hook.

How to Protect Yourself

Check first: one unsafe investment is all it takes to cripple you financially. Do not let anyone pressure you into making decisions about money or securities investments without getting independent financial advice. Protect yourself by learning to ask the right questions.

Here is a checklist of information you should get from any individual or company offering you a securities investment:

- What are your qualifications?
- Are you and your firm registered with a securities regulator?
- How long has your firm been in business?
- How long have you been with the firm?
- What is your education and professional experience?
- What products and services do you offer?
- How will you help me reach my goals?
- How are you paid for your services (salary, commission, or flat fee)?
- Can you provide me with references from clients who are like me or have participated in the investment you're offering?

Ask for written information about the company or investment. This may include:

- a prospectus
- an offering memorandum
- the most recent Annual Financial Report
- the most recent quarterly or interim financial reports
- recent news releases
- research reports prepared by the dealer/advisor
- examples of the statements you will receive
- information outlining the level of risk involved with the investment
- asking what exemption they may or may not be offering the investment under
- asking how you will be able to get your money back out at a

later date (e.g., can you sell what you've bought to someone else?)

Some final tips

- Never sign any paperwork that affects your finances or your home unless you clearly understand the implication of what you are signing. You may also want to consider hiring a lawyer to help review documents.
- Walk away from any lender who tries to pressure you into making a quick, spur-of-the-moment decision.
- Be cautious. Even when dealing with what appear to be trustworthy lenders, carefully consider more than one opportunity, because the terms of varying offers can differ significantly.

What Can I Do If I Think I Have Been Scammed?

If you have been approached about a seminar or real estate investment that doesn't seem right, or if you have invested money and now feel it is a scam, you can find out the process for making a complaint with your provincial securities commission and real estate council on their websites.

Speak out by talking about the investment with others. You may be able to help protect other family and friends who were thinking about getting involved.

Sarah's story

About two years ago, a reader emailed me asking for help. She had recently refinanced her home for approximately $150,000. At the time, her mortgage broker approved her for much more based on the value of her home and suggested that she take out an additional $100,000 line of credit on her mortgage and use that to invest in an "unbelievable" investment that the mortgage broker was also personally invested in. With no research or further questioning of the broker, Sarah decided to go ahead and take on the extra debt and investment. The mortgage broker wasn't selling the investment, but did recommend it. She also sold Sarah on the concept that since interest rates were so low and because she could deduct the interest on the line of credit since it was being used for an investment, the investment would literally pay for itself and the extra payments on the line of credit. This sounded good to Sarah and she signed on the mortgage and, later, the investment's dotted line.

At first, Sarah was receiving regular monthly payments from her investment, which, to her delight, more than covered her line of credit payment. A few months later, they just covered her payment. Just a few months after that, they stopped coming in altogether. Soon, she received a worrisome letter from the company telling her, among other things, that the founder had disappeared. Sarah's heart sank: she knew she had made a huge mistake.

Where did Sarah go wrong?

1. First, she trusted a mortgage broker (whom I hope she takes action against) on investment advice. I believe most mortgage brokers to be ethical individuals, but this was a massive breach of trust. Sarah was in the vulnerable position of getting a new mortgage and believed that the broker was acting in her best interest by recommending the extra line of credit for investment purposes. However, the broker's push to have Sarah take on more debt was likely just to increase the broker's totals that month (more credit extended to clients means more commissions to her). The mortgage broker was well within her rights to present the idea of Sarah's using extra funds to invest; however, she should have recommended Sarah first talk to a certified financial professional and a tax professional. She should never have had Sarah agree to such a complex and risky

strategy because she was likely confused by the whole mort-gage process at the time. The mortgage broker should also not have lead Sarah by recommending an investment that she was personally involved in without advising further counsel.

2. Now it's not all the broker's fault. Sarah's net worth at the time was about $150,000. Her home was worth approximately $300,000 and she had no other savings. Sarah admitted to me that she was a bit greedy and the proposition sounded great! What did she have to lose? She also admitted that she should have done some research and now was hoping I could get her money back.

3. Why would Sarah not spend even ten minutes researching an investment and strategy that was worth nearly as much as her total net worth? And how could she invest the total amount, and borrowed funds to boot, in an investment that she didn't even Google or understand? She had a hard time even explaining to me what the investment was.

4. Within a few seconds on Google, I found a litany of citations and warnings about the fraudsters Sarah trusted (not the mort-gage broker). Actually, there was a warning from the BC Secu-rities Commission released about two months before Sarah had invested. Had she spent just two minutes researching this per-fect investment, she would have discovered that the people in-volved in this investment were already being investigated out west.

Will Sarah be able to recoup her funds? It's doubtful and very unlikely. And even though Sarah approached me, she was unwilling to do much at all herself to recoup her investment. She wasn't willing to contact the mortgage broker, let alone report her. She didn't respond to the class action notification that other duped investors (and their lawyers) sent to her through the mail. Her only action was to contact me in the hope that I had a miracle up my sleeve.

If you or someone you know has been defrauded, it can be devastating. I've heard the outcries of many across Canada, but there is only so much the RCMP, securities commissions, and other agencies can do after the fact. The only way you as a consumer can protect yourself is to do as much research and due diligence as possible before you invest. It's not a guarantee and to be sure, even financial pros in the world could be fooled by a future Madoff. However, when it comes to matters of finance, you should never trust anyone completely with your hard-earned dollars. As I've said before, if you don't fully understand it, if it isn't presented in writing so you can have other professionals (such as tax, legal, etc.) give you a second opinion, don't sign on the dotted line!

Misleading Sales Tactics and Practices

Affinity fraud—In this situation salespeople are hired to target specific religious, ethnic, professional, or social groups. Once a prominent member of the group invests, more people within the community decide that the product is worthwhile. Having gained the community's trust, the salesperson then promotes the fraudulent products or services to the group at large.

Bait and switch schemes—Investors should be wary of investments that are advertised as having unusually high returns, especially if a personal visit is required. During the face-to-face meeting, the salesperson will discourage the investor from investing in the advertised product, switching them to a different investment altogether.

Churning—Churning occurs when a securities professional

makes unnecessary and/or excessive trades in order to generate commissions. Most churning occurs when an investor grants his or her broker discretion to trade the account on his or her behalf.

Guaranteed returns—Some investors may be enticed by promises of sky-high returns as they attempt to catch up on retirement planning or lost savings. Registered brokers and financial advisors are prohibited from guaranteeing a rate of return on securities products and/or minimizing risk.

Free meal seminars—Investors are invited to receive a free meal and hear about investment opportunities. While free meal seminars may be a legitimate method by which to obtain new clients, some seminar salespeople may try to sell you unsuitable investments or convince you to replace your existing investments. They may also fail to disclose their fees or commissions, making it difficult to accurately compare products and services. Others may use these seminars simply to obtain your personal and financial information.

Misleading credentials—Some salespeople or financial advisors create the impression that they have special education or expertise in senior/retirement services. If credentials contain words such as "senior" or "retirement" in conjunction with the words "certified" or "registered," be cautious. These credentials may be no more than a commercial gimmick. Their specialty may be more about knowing how to "sell" to seniors, and less about what may actually be in their clients' best interests.

UNREGISTERED ACTIVITY

Brokers/financial advisors - Would you trust your physical health to an unlicensed physician? Then why trust your financial well-being to an unregistered securities "professional"? Dealers and advisors are required to be registered with local and federal regulators.

Investment products—Some investment products must be registered with the provincial regulator where they are offered and sold. Always check with your advisor or regulator to make sure your investment funds are being placed in a legitimate investment product.

Navigating the Financial Industry

The financial industry is filled with men and women who are honest, ethical, experienced, educated, and truly wish to change people's lives by assisting them with their finances. However, as with any industry, there are always a few unethical individuals who ruin the reputation of others in the same business. The financial industry is tightly regulated with many checks and balances, even more so now than when I started in the industry. Clients are often frustrated with all of the paperwork that they must sign when making changes to their investments; however, these measures are in place to protect investors. Your investment advisor should be clearly disclosing the following to you: fees (hidden and otherwise), the investment risks and if there are any guarantees, the statements you'll receive about your investments and when, levels of service, options for selling, and more. I'm really not sure how, but each year and sometimes more than once, some shyster misappropriates or outright steals their clients' money and it hits the front page of the business section. More times than not, the client could have prevented the theft by reading the paperwork they signed and never totally trusting anyone with their money.

For the average consumer, "financial professional" can be an extremely confusing occupation. There are so many titles, designations and companies with unique positions. Whether it's a wealth manager who really specializes in life insurance and life insurance investments or the difficult-to-define "financial consultant," which can mean anything from a broker to a banker, you need to empower yourself before entering into a relationship.

There's nothing wrong with letting your current advisor know that you're making it a priority to educate yourself about your finances and although you might never formally have interviewed them before, you'd like to do it now. Be sure when you're looking for an advisor or evaluating your current one, that you always, I can't stress this enough, shop around. You can't fully assess the competencies, expertise, or your comfort level with this person requiring so much trust until you have experience with a few other individuals. Advisors are businesspeople. Don't take the relationship personally and stay with someone who continually under performs, makes you feel uncomfortable, or simply doesn't value your business because they're a friend, you've been with them forever, or it's your brother's son. Your money and financial security is a business matter for you as well. Ensure you're comfortable with your professional, but otherwise check emotions at the door.

You also need an interview checklist for your current or new advisor. Use the following as a start and ask your friends and network what questions they've asked their advisors. If your advisor is taken aback by this questioning (they should actually be offering a checklist of their own before you ask), doesn't answer any of your questions, or provides some vague responses, don't go back. It's that simple.

YOUR FINANCIAL TEAM

I encourage you to assemble your financial team now and as the need arises. Generally, it does not cost you anything for an initial consultation, which you should consider setting up, even if you think the product or service does not apply to your current situation. Shop around and if you need a referral, ask friends and family who they are using. Also, if you have at least one of the following professionals that you use (i.e., your banker), ask them to introduce you to their preferred advisors. You'll find them quick to assist with a list of names and they likely have a good idea of the quality of those professionals. Keep in mind that whether you were referred or not, use the questionnaire later in this chapter to assist you and always shop around.

Banker —This individual should help you with your day-to-day banking, lending, and possibly investing.

Financial advisor—They should equip you with a written financial plan. A financial advisor may charge for this if you do not invest with them. If you do they will likely provide a plan for free. This professional could work at a bank, brokerage, independent firm, or life insurance company. Remember to ask what they are licensed to sell, as the title "financial advisor" can apply to many different types of professionals.

Fee-only Certified Financial Planner—They are gaining in popularity, but there is still only a small minority of financial professionals who work in this manner. They don't sell or offer any products or investments. You would simply hire them to take a look at your total financial, retirement, tax, and estate-planning situation for a fee—anywhere from $500–$2,000. In Canada, we're not used to paying these types of fees for planning advice and I suspect that's the only reason these professionals are in the minority. After all, many financial advisors and brokers will provide you with a plan as a loss leader when you invest with them. However, a fee only CFP will look at much more than your investments, like paying down your debt, and your total plan picture, and without the hidden agenda of selling you an investment. There are many excellent advisors who will provide a free plan for you, however, I highly recommend hiring a fee only CFP once every five or ten years, even if you are working with an advisor of some type. See my site for resources that will help you find a fee only CFP in your area.

Life insurance agent—These professionals will, at no charge, provide you with an insurance analysis, including life insurance coverage, critical illness insurance, and disability insurance. More on insurance can be found in Chapter 7.

General insurance agent—These agents handle auto and home policies. If you're self-employed, inquire about errors and omissions and/or liability coverage.

Lawyer—Look for a legal professional who specializes in what you need. Seek counsel for your estate plan at any stage in your life. There are many legal professionals who work only in the areas of estate planning. You'll wish to use their skills to draft your will, powers of attorney, living wills, and more. If you're self-employed, consult a lawyer and accountant to learn about the benefits of incorporating your company.

Accountant—Depending on the complexity of your financial situation and whether you're employed or self-employed, you may need the services of a qualified accountant. However, if your tax situation is simple, a tax preparer might suffice.

How Do I Find the Right Investment Advisor?

Finding the right advisor is important, so take the time to choose one who has the necessary qualifications, experience and, as important, is someone with whom you feel comfortable. After all you don't want just anyone helping you manage your money and your future.

WHERE DO I START?

Ask for referrals. Your friends, family or work associates may have financial advisors, but never assume that someone who's right for them is right for you.

Check first and make sure the individual is registered to sell investments. You can check if an individual or firm is registered to sell investments with your provincial securities commission, and various governing bodies. For a complete list, please visit my website.

Also check to see if this person has been disciplined in another jurisdiction by reviewing the CSA Disciplined Persons List, which can be found on the Canadian Securities Administrators' website.

NEXT STEPS

Once you have a list of potential advisors, contact them for a brief telephone interview. If you like what you hear, move on to an in-person interview where you'll ask more detailed questions. A potential advisor should be able to provide you with a few references; talk to them before you make your final choice.

Step 1: Phone First!

Talking to potential advisors over the phone can help you reduce your list and decide which ones you'd like to meet. Use the following questions to help you narrow your search:

- Are you registered to sell investments? What type(s)?
- What are your formal qualifications?
- How much experience do you have?
- What types of clients do you have?
- How many clients do you have?
- What hours do you work and when are you not available?

You may want to use the AdvisorReport service of IIROC (Investment Industry Regulatory Organization of Canada)—it's free and can help you research the professional backgrounds of current IIROC-registered advisors. You can find a link on my site.

Step 2: Meet Potential Advisors

Once you've narrowed down your list, it's time for a face-to-face meeting. Keep the interview relatively short (about half-an-hour should do) and stick to the topics at hand. It's recommended that you ask the advisor questions like these:

- Describe your formal qualifications. What do they involve?
- What types of investments are you registered to sell?
- Are you restricted to certain companies in the products you offer? If so, what companies are they?
- How are you paid?
- How often will you contact me?
- What is your investment philosophy?
- Will you be handling my account personally or do you have an assistant?
- Can you provide me with references from your existing client base?

You may also want to conduct a background check to determine if there has been any enforcement action against the firm or individual offering the investment.

Step 3: Talk To References

Calling references is a great way to learn more about a potential advisor and to confirm any suspicions that may have arisen from your in-person meeting. The following questions can help you learn even more about a potential advisor.

- How long has your advisor worked with you?
- How satisfied are you with his/her services?
- What are his/her strong points? Weak points?
- Does your advisor have any special areas of expertise?

- Have you ever been disappointed or surprised by anything in your relationship with your advisor?
- How often do you hear from him/her regarding your investments?
- Who normally initiates the calls?
- How quickly are your calls returned?

WORKING TOGETHER

Your relationship with your advisor is not one-sided. It is, after all, your money, and you're in control. There are a few things you can expect a good advisor to do for you, and there are several things you can do to ensure your relationship with your advisor is productive.

You can expect your advisor to:

- Know their clients, also known as KYC. (Advisors will often have a know your client form.)
- Behave in an ethical, honest manner
- Fully disclose all risks
- Make personalized recommendations

You should:
- Have a clear understanding of your values, your goals, and your wishes in life—both short- and long-term.
- Have clear expectations about what you want your advisor to do.

CHANGING ADVISORS

Your relationship with your advisor is intended to be long-term. You're in it for the long haul. But it's okay to make a change if you find your needs have changed. If you do change advisors and the new one suggests switching products, ask questions about fees, the respective long-term performance of your current portfolio, and the product(s) he/she is recommending. Also ask about potential compensation for him/her should you switch. Make sure it makes sense for you, not just for your advisor.

MORE INFORMATION

Contact professional associations for assistance or information. You can contact the organizations below with your questions:

- Financial Planning Standards Council (FPSC)
- The Financial Advisors Association of Canada (Advocis)
- Investment Industry Regulatory Organization of Canada (IIROC)
- Mutual Fund Dealers Association (MFDA)
- Investment Counsel Association of Canada
- Montreal Exchange—Approved Participants
- TMX Group (Toronto Stock Exchange and TSX Venture Exchange)

If you want information on:

- Portfolio Managers, Investment Counsel, Scholarship Plan Dealers, and/or Securities Advisors—contact provincial or territorial securities commission
- Mutual Fund Dealers—contact the MFDA or your provincial or territorial securities commission
- Investment Dealers (Brokers)—contact IIROC

Recap

- There are crooks out there—learn strategies to protect yourself
- Never trust someone completely with your finances

- Do your own research before asking advice
- Don't be afraid to shop around
- Create a checklist of questions to ask professionals
- Know in brief what a professional's designations are and what services/products they are allowed to sell or provide. Ask about their personal bias so you can make an informed decision about using their services.

HELPFUL INVESTOR RESOURCES

Canadian Securities Administrators
www.securities-administrators.ca/
British Columbia Securities Commission - www.bcsc.bc.ca/
Alberta Securities Commission - www.albertasecurities.com
Manitoba Securities Commission - www.msc.gov.mb.ca/
Saskatchewan Financial Services Commission
www.sfsc. gov.sk.ca/
Quebec AMF - www.lautorite.qc.ca
Ontario Securities Commission - www.osc.gov.on.ca/
New Brunswick Securities Commission - www.nbsc-cvmnb.ca/
Nova Scotia Securities Commission - www.gov.ns.ca/nssc/
PEI Securities Office - www.gov.pe.ca/securities/
Yukon Securities Registry –
www.community. gov.yk.ca/corp/secureinvest.html
Northwest Territories Securities Office
www.justice.gov. nt.ca/SecuritiesRegistry/index.shtml
Nunavut Securities Office
www.justice.gov.nu.ca/i18n/english/legreg/sr_index.shtm

The following titles from this chapter as listed are reprinted by permission of the Alberta Securities Commission, all rights reserved. "Scam Sensor," "Red Flag Alert – Questions to Ask Yourself of the Seller," "Investor Watch," "Ponzi Schemes," "Pyramid Schemes," "Pump & Dump," "Investment Clubs," "Scam Marketing," "Real Estate Investment Opportunities," "Commonly Used Promotion Tactics," "Real Estate Investment Seminars," "Check First," "Spot the Red Flags of Unsafe Securities Investments," "How to Protect Yourself," "What Can I Do If I Think I Have Been Scammed," "Misleading Sales Tactics & Practices," "Unregistered Activity," and "How Do I Find the Right Investment Advisor?"

Chapter 5

Tax Shelters

Quick Quiz

1. RRSPs and RRIFs are actual investments.

True ☐

False ☐

2. Interest on an RRSP loan is tax deductible.

True ☐

False ☐

3. A Tax-Free Savings Account is best suited for investors who are:

A. Extremely high risk

B. Extremely low risk

C. New to investing; they don't make much sense and offer a low rate of return

D. Nearly all investors could benefit from a TFSA

4. Non-registered investments grow tax free.

True ☐

False ☐

5. Investments producing capital gains, interest income, or dividends are all taxed at the same rate.

True ☐

False ☐

The financial industry has done a superb job of educating investors about the tax and growth benefits of RRSPs. These shelters, along with others offered by the Canadian government, as we'll discover, can be a great option for many. However, there are quite a few misconceptions about how these shelters work, when they're right for you, and when other options might be better. Let's delve into the not-so-exciting, but potentially tax saving world of tax shelters.

Non-Registered and Registered Investments

When I worked in the financial industry and today when I lecture on investments, I'm shocked that so many individuals think an RRSP is a type of investment. When a client would complain about their RRSP portfolios and I'd ask them what was in their RRSP, they would always have a perplexed look and would usually say something like, "It's an RRSP." They withheld the word "stupid" at the end of their statement, I'm sure. Even today, I'll ask audiences if an RRSP is an investment, and most will shake their heads yes.

In fact, RRSPs and other shelters we'll look at are not investments. They're tax shelters. I like to think of them as garages: you still need to put cars in your garage. An RRSP or Registered Retirement Savings Plan is just an empty vessel with tax incentives offered by the government. To open an RRSP at a bank, with a broker, or financial advisor, there's a simple form that's filled out and then you can have as many RRSPs as you'd like (with different banks for example, one with a broker, etc.). I'll go through the inner workings in a moment.

Let's go back to the garage analogy. Let's say you open an RRSP with your bank. You deposit $5,000 and fill out a form. Maybe it's a busy time of year and you make it in just before the deadline. Your banker encourages you to simply "park" the funds in a cash account and for you both to get together after the rush of the RRSP season. This scenario happens all the time and all too often, unfortunately, the investor and advisor don't properly allocate those funds.

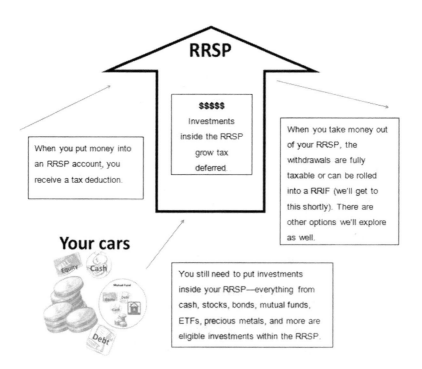

RRSP

$$$$$
Investments inside the RRSP grow tax deferred.

When you put money into an RRSP account, you receive a tax deduction.

When you take money out of your RRSP, the withdrawals are fully taxable or can be rolled into a RRIF (we'll get to this shortly). There are other options we'll explore as well.

Your cars

You still need to put investments inside your RRSP—everything from cash, stocks, bonds, mutual funds, ETFs, precious metals, and more are eligible investments within the RRSP.

DEFINITION CHECK

An RRSP is a tax shelter, but not an invest-  Definition check

ment. When you put money into an RRSP, you get a tax deduction. It grows tax free during the life of the plan, and you're taxed when you take it out (we'll look at that shortly).

What's the main difference between an RRSP and a regular investment that isn't within a tax shelter (called a non-registered account)? The difference is the tax treatment. If your "cars" or investments are bought and held outside a tax shelter, the interest is subject to tax each year, as are the capital gains when they're sold. However, you're also free to do what you wish with them since the tax is paid each year (for example, you could gift those funds to a spouse or child, whereas you couldn't with an RRSP). If those exact same "cars" or investments were held inside an RRSP, you have to adhere to the rules of the RRSP (for instance, if an RRSP holder passes away, they can give or "roll over" those funds to a spouse tax free, but if there is no spouse those funds are fully taxable at the time of death).

RRSPs vs. Non-registered Assets (also called "open accounts")

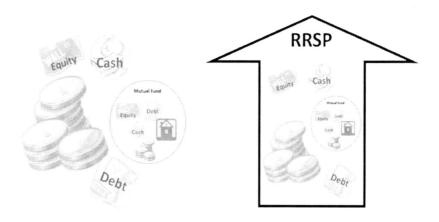

Non-Registered Assets	RRSP
• You're taxed each year on the interest that you earn.	• You get a tax deduction for your contribution.
• With stocks or real estate for example, you're taxed on the capital gain when you sell (see Page 96) and only 50% is taxable at your marginal tax rate (federal and provincial taxes combined). If you bought a stock last year for $2,000 and sold it the following year for $2,500, you would have a capital gain of $500. You're only taxed on $250, so you pay tax, at your marginal tax bracket, on $250.	• Your investments grow tax deferred (you don't pay tax until you take the money out). • There's quite a bit of flexibility in how you take your money out: in annual payments in a RRIF (we'll discuss shortly), as a loan of sorts to yourself with the Home Buyers' Plan, if you're going back to school, or if you're out of work and have little to no income.
• Because you pay tax regularly on these investments, you're free to gift them or cash them out. Upon	• If you and/or your spouse will have a sizable pension at retirement, RRSPs might not be the best option, as you're forced to

your death your heirs wouldn't pay tax upon receiving them (this is a general rule without getting into too much taxation).

• Investments that are more tax preferred, such as those producing a capital gain or dividend, should be held outside of an RRSP.

• You're not forced to take your investments out of a non-registered portfolio like with an RRSP—again, because you've paid tax yearly or regularly on them.

take a certain amount out of your RRIF plan at retirement. The extra income, added to a pension, could force you into a higher tax bracket.

• The theory and benefit to RRSPs is not only the tax deduction, but that your investments will grow more over time than they would outside of an RRSP, because the tax is deferred.

RRSPs—The Ins and Outs

• You're allowed to contribute 18% of income earned the previous year to your RRSP. If you have a pension, this amount is reduced and is called a PA (pension adjustment). The deadline is March 1 to make contributions for the previous year.

Robert had $52,000 of earned income in 2010. He's eligible to make a contribution of up to $9,360. He hasn't saved that amount, but decides to get a RRSP loan. He has to make his contribution by March 1, 2011, to get the deduction on his 2010 tax return. This year, Robert's going to start saving monthly so he doesn't have to take out a loan. Plus, if he does that, his savings will grow quicker because they're deferring tax by getting into an RRSP monthly. He'll also take advantage of dollar cost averaging by buying investments such as stocks or equity mutual funds, instead of putting his $9,360 in on a given day hoping that the markets are low on that day. By purchasing monthly, he takes advantage of buying at various times during the year, which generally works to an investor's advantage.

- You receive a tax deduction based on your marginal tax bracket. A general guideline is to multiply your marginal tax bracket (your provincial and federal tax rate) by the amount you're contributing.

Jessie earned $30,000 this year and has a marginal tax rate of 26%. She's thinking of contributing $3,000 to an RRSP, which will generate a tax deduction of $780. There are many factors that account for the exact deduction you'll receive, but my calculation will give you a good idea as to what you can expect as a tax deduction. But remember, the tax refund is not free money. It's money that the government has been withholding from you without interest. Use your tax refund wisely and remember that's it's your money, not a windfall.

- The maximum you could contribute in 2010 was $22,000 (the maximum has increase by $1,000 a year since 2007). There's a lifetime over-contribution limit of $2,000. If you exceed that, there's a penalty for doing so.

Jake's earned income has generally hovered around $65,000 for the past ten years and he's not anticipating it will increase much in the future. However, he sold a rental property this year and has a hefty capital gain. It's an unusual year for him income wise (due to the sale of the property) and he's not likely to experience it again. He's been moved into a new tax bracket because of capital gains on the sale of his rental property. He should talk to his accountant about using the $2,000 over contribution this year because it's the one year that he'll receive the highest tax deduction

- If you don't use your maximum allowable amount, you can carry it forward to future years. See the blue tax forms that comes in the mail after you've filed your tax return. You'll see a box with the total amount you're allowed to contribute.

Caroline's been working part-time during her university years and never had the extra cash to put into an RRSP. Plus, every dollar of income was needed to pay down her debt. She's finally working full time and this year she's expected to have over $65,000 of earned income. Should she talk to her banker and accountant to see if it makes sense to take out a RRSP loan and take advantage of all of her "unused room," or should she spread it out over a few years now that her income has started to increase dramatically?

- You can delay claiming the tax deduction if a future year may benefit more.

Lisa received a $25,000 gift from her parents, but she's on maternity leave and has very little earned income this year. She has her debts paid off and wants to start saving for retirement. She'd like to take advantage of the tax deferment of an RRSP because the tax deduction for contributing now will be negligible. She plans on getting back to her $70,000+ salary next year, so, her advisor suggests she contributes now, but defers the deduction until the year she has significantly more income.

- You can open as many RRSPs as you'd like and transfer within them.

Carl has three RRSP plans: A group one from work, one at his bank, and a plan with his financial advisor. He can't move his group plan yet, but the other two are creating a paperwork annoyance for him, and he's not sure if all his eggs are in the same basket. He decides to consolidate everything with a new financial planner and is able to move the bank RRSP and the other from his old financial advisor to the new one. The mutual funds he has in his RRSP at the bank are commission free. However, those with his financial advisor have some deferred sales charge commissions left on them if he leaves the mutual fund family that they're in. He can negotiate with the old financial advisor to see if those fees can be reduced, or he can talk to the new financial advisor and move those funds and the RRSP over "in-kind." In the latter situation, everything is moved over "as is," it's just under the direction of his new advisor and merged with the RRSP from his bank. Since none of the funds are sold, there is no commission paid. Once the old commissions drop off, he and his new advisor can see if more suitable investments would make more sense for his portfolio. He's also getting all hidden and other fees in writing before he makes any decisions in the future—he wasn't aware of the fees for leaving his old financial advisor.

• At death, you can roll your RRSP over to a spouse tax free, but it's fully taxable to anyone else (other than in circumstances with certain dependants).

Kathy's mom recently passed away; her dad died years ago. She's an only child and her mom had a RRIF worth $267,000. (We'll examine RRIFs shortly.) Even though Kathy was named as a beneficiary under the RRIF plan, Kathy's mom's estate will have to pay the tax. And because the entire amount ($267,000) will be included as income along with any other income she had that year, Kathy's mom's estate and the RRIF will be subject to the highest tax bracket and tax payable. (It would work the same if she was under age 71 and still had an RRSP.)

DEFINITION CHECK

Home Buyers' Plan

To encourage Canadians to save, our government has made investing in RRSPs more flexible over the years by including the option to use your RRSP as a down payment for your first home.

The maximum amount you can borrow is $25,000 and it has to be paid back (to your RRSP plan) within 15 years. If you don't, the RRSP room that you used is lost forever. You also can't have owned a home in the last five years; that's the criteria for being considered a "new home buyer."

Lifelong Learning Plan

Another wonderfully flexible option with RRSPs is the ability to use the funds for your own education. It's called the Lifelong Learning Plan and it also allows you to withdraw a maximum of $20,000 to help you pay tuition. You can only withdraw $10,000 a year. Repayment doesn't have to commence until five years after the first withdrawal and you have ten years to pay back the full amount. Similar to the Home Buyers' Program, if you fail to do that, your RRSP "room" and the opportunity to pay yourself back is lost for good.

CASE STUDIES

Niles and Sophie

Niles and Sophie live in Ontario and earn $52,000 and $58,000 a year respectively. Neither have a pension. They're planning to purchase a home in the near future, but have nothing saved up as yet. They're wondering if they'd be better off to invest in an RRSP and use the Home Buyers' Plan option in a few years when they're ready, or if they should save outside of an RRSP. They're wondering if the tax deduction makes it worthwhile. They also have a car loan for $10,000 at an 8% interest rate and one credit card with a balance of $2,000 and a 12.5% interest rate. They have $5,000 each to invest in an RRSP.

Should Niles and Sophie:
1. Pay off the loan?
2. Pay off the credit card and part of the loan?
3. Invest in an RRSP and use the Home Buyers' Plan later?
4. Save outside of an RRSP?

Objective: To buy their first home using the most financially feasible method, while minimizing taxes.

Present summary: Family income of $110,000 with $12,000 in debt, $10,000 annual surplus funds, no savings or pension, and are looking to buy in the next few years.

Suggested strategy: Niles and Sophie are in a pretty good position to shop around as long as they can qualify for a mortgage. Given time is on their side, the two things they should do are find a good real estate agent who will find a motivated seller with a home they like and get pre-approved for a mortgage (when they're ready to shop), which they can use to jump on any deals they might find right away. They should also scope out a well-recommended home inspector and an appraiser who can help them determine if they are buying a good property and if the numbers works in their favour.

Once they purchase, they will likely need to put a few thousand into immediate repairs and furnishing, so there will be at least a $10,000 cash outlay. The home inspector will be able to give a better idea of the cost of repairs and an idea of when they should be addressed.

There are a number of possible options that Niles and Sophie can pursue. They need to sit down with a financial advisor, accountant, or a fee-only certified financial planner. Sometimes crunching the numbers makes a decision crystal clear and sometimes it becomes more muddled. The best course of action depends on current and future tax situations, rates of investments vs. debt, and, of course, some luck (number and projections are helpful, but without knowing what interest and investment rates will do, there's certainly some guess work involved).

Some obvious considerations for them to talk with a professional about include:

- The RRSP is a good idea since their $10,000 investment (based on the their marginal tax brackets) will generate a tax deduction of $3,124. That's 31% back from the government not factoring in the growth of the plan. They can do this for two years (up to $20,000) with the Home Buyers' Plan.

After the second year they will need to figure out with their professionals:

- When they want to purchase their home
- The approximate price, what they can get approved for, the monthly payments they're comfortable with, and therefore what down payment they need.

After year two, they need to determine if investing in the RRSP is still the best option or if they should use a tax-free savings account. It would be a tax detriment to invest more than the Home Buyers' Plan would allow into an RRSP and then have to take it out for the down payment (remember, RRSPs are taxed when funds are withdrawn).

Based on the high interest rates of their loan and credit card, they may wish to allocated the extra funds in year three and four to pay off their high interest debt and free up cash flow for the mortgage payments. They hopefully also reduced this debt in year one and two by using the tax refund to pay down this debt.

Here's how the next few years will go:

- Put all $10,000 towards RRSPs the first year—they'll need the down payment when the bargain shows up. The taxman will give them about $3K in refunds for investing in their RRSPs, which they should use to start paying off their debts.
- Keep building the RRSP fund until they find the right property. Remember, they're not desperate to buy, so unless a good bargain shows up, they should keep going with their saving plan.
- Once they land the property, they should pay off the car loan and credit card with tax refunds or money left over from the house deal. Because they don't know when they'll land it, I can't say how much will be left over and when. But the bottom line here is that there should be a definite strategy in place, which the couple can start implementing immediately, allowing them to move at the right time.

What to look for and avoid:

- Don't fall in love with any deal unless the numbers all make sense. Find a realtor who's been recommend by your professional team and call for references. Avoid one who is working for both the seller and buyer: they'll sign a disclosure agreement, but it's nearly impossible to work in the interest of both.

- Consider a property that is marketable rather than a dream home. Bungalows under 2,000 square feet or two to three bedroom condos in working class neighbourhoods are good examples of properties that people buy in any market. Statistics show that first-time home buyers move after five to ten years, so they will want their equity as portable as possible. Also keep the property you are buying in the mid- to low-price range, so the maintenance costs are along that same line.

Closing comments

First time home buying is as much a romantic experience as it is challenging. Always remember that the honeymoon does end faster than you think and you have to be prepared when the reality of maintenance, payments, and learning the homeowner ropes sets in after a few weeks. Not only it is important that Niles and Sophie build a list of experts who will help them, they must be focused on their priorities in order for their long-term plan to succeed. Where most couples go wrong is they over extend in what they buy and they are too unrealistic with their budgets (if one even exists or is being followed). A financial planner and tax professional can help here, but really it is up to the couple to determine that they stick to the plan; it is this that will ultimately make or break them.

Jackson

Based on Jackson's situation below, should he make any changes or is he on the right track?

Non-registered portfolio (no shelter—just investments bought on their own) with the follow assets:
- A bond fund
- Some shares in a few bank stocks
- An 18-month GIC
- A modest emergency fund sitting in a savings account (earning less than 1%)

The RRSP that he contributes the maximum to each year consists of:
- Several laddered GICs (he thinks he's a lower risk investor when it comes to his RRSP)
- Three mutual funds: one is a balanced fund (with stocks, bonds, and cash); one is a dividend fund; and one is an equity fund.

Debts

Jackson has a secured line of credit with a balance on it, but the interest rate is pretty low (under 4%) and a mortgage.

What three obvious changes should Jackson make and why?

1. _____
2. _____
3. _____

Were you able to spot all three and maybe even suggest more?

1. Jackson should move his asset mix around within the non-registered portfolio and RRSP as much as possible and look at the total amount when considering the investment mix. His risk tolerance shouldn't differ in an RRSP vs. non-registered investment (other than his emergency savings or monies for short-term use). He should hold as many of the capital gain earning investments and those earning dividends outside of the RRSP as possible and hold as much of those earning just income inside the RRSP (such as the bonds and GICs). Why? Because remember that stocks earning a capital gain or dividend have a preferred tax treatment. On a non-registered account, Jackson has to pay tax each year on the interest earned or on the capital gain when he sells his stocks. In the RRSP, annual tax treatment or type is irrelevant. All investments grow tax deferred and all are taxed the same way when withdrawn: as income.

2. He should pay off his line of credit with his emergency cash account. Why? First, he's paying a higher interest rate on the line of credit that he's carrying a balance on than he's earning in the cash account. Second, since you can easily withdraw from or pay down on a line of credit, as long as you're responsible with keeping the balance low or paid off, it's a great tool for dealing with emergencies, if they come up.

3. Did you think of the third thing he should do? It's a bit of a trick question, as I haven't covered this shelter yet. He should consider moving some of his assets to a tax-free savings account or at least think about allocating some of his future non-registered investments to one. He can go back as well and take advantage of unused room since the government introduced the plan.

RRIFs—Registered Retirement Income Funds

At the age of 71, you're required by the government to take action with your RRSP. You can:

- Roll it into a RRIF
- Cash it out fully or in part (this would be a tax nightmare for most RRSP holders, but it is an option)
- Purchase a life/term fixed annuity (remember, for a full list of definitions, visit my site at www.kelleykeehn.com/themoney book.html)

The most common choice is a RRIF. A RRIF is exactly like an RRSP, the only difference is that income is required to be withdrawn from it (either monthly, quarterly, or annually). Once you change your RRSP to a RRIF, you can not add any new funds to it, but the funds within the plan will still grow tax deferred. Why would someone want to convert to a RRIF? First, because the government requires you to do so by age 71. Basically, your investment has grown tax deferred over the years and a RRIF forces you to draw income from it, thus, the government finally has the opportunity to tax you on that income. Secondly, if an individual is retired under the age of 71, they may wish to start receiving a regular stream of income and can roll their RRSP into a RRIF early.

At RRIF time (before the end of the year in which you turn 71), it's as easy as filling out a simple form to transfer the RRSP into the new shelter. With a RRIF, all of the assets seamlessly roll over. If you have three plans for example at three different financial institutions, you would then need three RRIF plans. You could, however, depending on the investments within the plan, consolidate those accounts to one financial institution or leave them as separate plans. You can't add funds to a RRIF plan and you're forced to take at least a minimum amount out of the plan annually (it can be paid to you monthly or quarterly as well) and you can take more than the minimum any year, or even collapse the entire plan. But again, all those funds would be taxable, so withdrawing all of the plan's funds at once is not a viable option for most. All of the assets that remain in the RRIF continue to grow tax deferred.

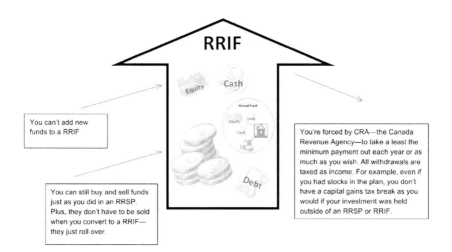

You can't add new funds to a RRIF

You can still buy and sell funds just as you did in an RRSP. Plus, they don't have to be sold when you convert to a RRIF—they just roll over.

You're forced by CRA—the Canada Revenue Agency—to take a least the minimum payment out each year or as much as you wish. All withdrawals are taxed as income. For example, even if you had stocks in the plan, you don't have a capital gains tax break as you would if your investment was held outside of an RRSP or RRIF.

A RRIF holder doesn't need to worry about the maturity of their investments come RRIF time or that they need to sell any of their assets just to roll their RRSP over to a RRIF. For example, if a 69-year-old buys a five-year GIC and a couple of stocks inside their RRSP, they would roll over two years later when the person turned 71. Even though there would be three years left on the GIC, everything would just be transferred. Again, it's a simple form that you complete at your bank, with your broker, or financial planner.

This table shows the minimum withdrawal rates set for RRIFs for 2007. Note that the rate really goes up starting at age 71.

Age at January 1st	Minimum withdrawal	Age at January 1st	Minimum withdrawal
65	4.00%	80	8.75%
66	4.17%	81	8.99%
67	4.35%	82	9.27%
68	4.55%	83	9.58%
69	4.76%	84	9.93%
70	5.00%	85	10.33%
71	7.38%	86	10.79%
72	7.48%	87	11.33%
73	7.59%	88	11.96%
74	7.71%	89	12.71%
75	7.85%	90	13.62%
76	7.99%	91	14.73%
77	8.15%	92	16.12%
78	8.33%	93	17.92%
79	8.53%	94+	20.00%

After age 94, the withdrawal rate stays at 20% until the account is empty.

Source: Ontario Securities Commission

A 74-year-old with a RRIF portfolio of $250,000 would have to withdraw a minimum of 7.71% or $19,275. No matter what the total return on the RRIF portfolio is each year, the withdrawal table is designed to eventually deplete the RRIF. You'll notice that the graph list ages earlier than the mandatory age 71 for RRIF payments. Just because the government forces an RRSP holder to convert at age 71, it doesn't mean that you couldn't do so earlier, say in the case of early retirement or if you simply wanted to withdraw the funds on a regular basis.

Although how you invest the "cars" within your RRIF "garage" can be consistent with how you were investing your RRSP plan (see Page 86 for asset allocation factors), a RRIF holder should consider having enough liquid, available assets for the annual RRIF withdrawal. If all of the holdings in the RRIF were in stocks, bonds, and a number of medium-risk mutual funds and the stock market dropped or the bond hasn't matured at withdrawal time, the investor may have to sell investments at the wrong time. Having some of the assets in the RRIF sold off at regular intervals (sort of dollar cost averaging—but this time with selling) is the best strategy for having those dollars available at withdrawal time.

What happens if you want to take out more than the minimum amount?

If you want to take out more than the minimum amount, your withdrawal will be subject to withholding tax. If you make a withdrawal from your RRSP or more than the minimum from your RRIF, the government requires the financial institution to withhold tax. The percent withheld depends on the size of the withdrawal. See below for rates. Even though taxes are withheld, depending on one's specific situation or the amount of income that person drew that year, more or less tax may be owed. It all depends on your tax situation and the amount of income you had for the year. The bank or financial institution is mandated by the government to withhold a certain amount of tax.

WITHHOLDING TAX TABLES

Withdrawals in excess of the minimum payment are subject to the following withholding tax rates: (withdrawal amount for residents of all provinces except Quebec)

Up to $5,000.00	10%
$5,000.01 to $15,000.00	20%
$15,000.01 and over	30%

RRSP vs. RRIF

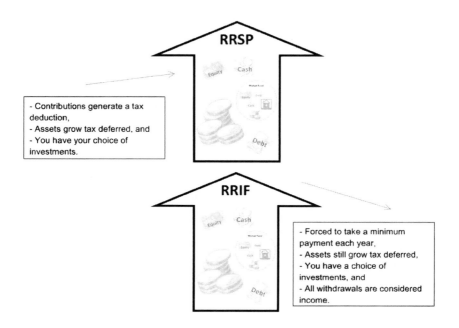

- Contributions generate a tax deduction,
- Assets grow tax deferred, and
- You have your choice of investments.

- Forced to take a minimum payment each year,
- Assets still grow tax deferred,
- You have a choice of investments, and
- All withdrawals are considered income.

TFSAs—Tax-Free Savings Accounts

This is the newest tax shelter that our government has introduced to encourage Canadians to save and for the very first time (that I can recall anyway), an investment can be called "tax free" (RRSP and RRIF funds are only tax deferred because tax is paid eventually).

Think of the TFSA as yet another garage. Investments held within this garage have different rules and guidelines. The TFSA was introduced by the government in January 2009 and most financial experts agree that TFSAs are great for just about every investor.

Under a TFSA, you're able to invest $5,000 per year. If you didn't take advantage of the program when it started, you can carry

the \$5,000/year room forward. For example, if, in 2011, you haven't yet invested in a TFSA, you could contribute \$15,000 (\$5,000 for each of the years since 2009 when it started). The funds inside the TFSA grow tax free and no tax is due when funds are withdrawn, gifted, or passed on at death.

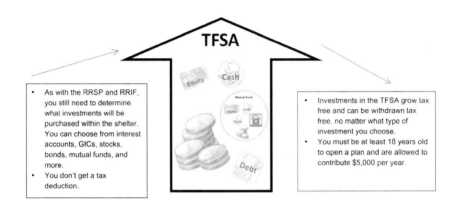

- As with the RRSP and RRIF, you still need to determine what investments will be purchased within the shelter. You can choose from interest accounts, GICs, stocks, bonds, mutual funds, and more.
- You don't get a tax deduction.

- Investments in the TFSA grow tax free and can be withdrawn tax free, no matter what type of investment you choose.
- You must be at least 18 years old to open a plan and are allowed to contribute \$5,000 per year.

RESP—Registered Education Savings Plan

The last Canadian tax shelter is the RESP. These plans, like the other I've discussed, can be purchased at a bank, with your broker, or a financial planner. The intention is to save for your child or grandchild's education. Again, funds inside any shelter have special rules and so does this shelter.

The popularity of this plan in due not only to the tax deferred savings (it's like the RRSP, but you don't get a tax deduction), you also get a government incentive called the Canadian Education Savings Grant—the CESG. The government matches 20% of the annual RESP contribution to a maximum of \$500 per year and \$7,200 in the child's lifetime. There's also no longer a maximum annual contribution: it's now a simple \$50,000 lifetime limit per child, also called a beneficiary.

There are individual and family plans. The latter allows you to share the plan with other beneficiaries (your children) in case one doesn't go to a qualified post-secondary institution.

The RESP assets grow tax deferred and are taxed in the child's hands when they withdraw them for qualified post-secondary educational purposes. The additional benefit is that the child usually has little to no income while going to school, so the taxes eventually paid will be minimal.

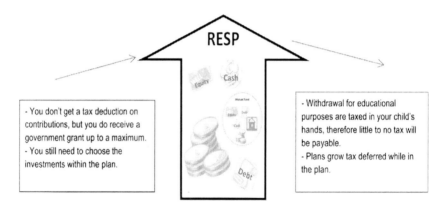

What happens if your child doesn't go to school?

There are a number of options including:

- You can choose another beneficiary in a family plan
- Take all of it in cash—this option would be subject to income tax on the money earned in the plan (but not what you contributed) and a 20% penalty (because of the grant)
- Transfer it to your own RRSP (you'd need to have the contribution room to do so) up to $50,000.

It's difficult for many parents of young children to know if their child will want to pursue higher learning or not. However, most financial experts would agree that RESPs and the government incentives make it a worthwhile investment option for education savings even if your child later chooses not to pursue a post-secondary education.

DEFINITION CHECK

Self-directed accounts—This applies to any registered account, including RRSPs, RRIFs, TFSAs, and RESPs. Basically, if you opened up an account with a bank or financial planner, you would have a number of investment choices at  your disposal, such as interest bearing accounts, GICs with your bank, mutual and index funds, and more. If you would like to include individual securities (along with the investments just listed), such as stocks, bonds, ETFs, and more, then you would need to open a self-directed account either with a broker (each bank has a brokerage arm) or online with your banker, broker, or advisor.

Foreign Content Rules

This used to be a major issue with registered plans and limits have bounced around over the years. Today, there are no foreign content limits, so an investor is free to allocate their money to any mix of investments, even if they're comprised of holdings outside of Canada (for example, a Far East Mutual Fund or US Equity Fund).

FURTHER READING NOT COVERED IN THIS CHAPTER

LIRAs (Locked-in Retirement Accounts) and LRSPs (Locked-in Retirement Savings Plans)—A LIRA or LRSP was at one point a company pension and thus is governed by pension regulations. LIRAs or LRSPs allow account holders to control the investments themselves. However, unlike with an RRSP/RRIF, you cannot make a withdrawal at any time.

LRIFs (Locked-in Retirement Income Funds) and LIFs (Life Income Funds)—These are what your LIRA or LRSP become at maturity, depending on which province you live in. Just as a RRSP has to be converted to a RRIF, so does an LIRA and LRSP need to be converted to a LRIF or LIF. Again, the process and name depends on the province where the account was set up. Unlike RRIFs, LIFs and LRIFs have a minimum and maximum amount that can be withdrawn each year. The reason there's a maximum is that these plans were originally considered pensions of some sort and therefore follow pension guidelines. The intent is that the funds are to last the lifetime of the account holder, so it can't just be depleted in a given year.

Annuities—There are many types of annuities—fixed and life—with many options within each. A life annuity, for example, works opposite to a mortgage. Your total investment is divided up to you over your lifetime based on a current interest rate. Estimates of the investor's lifespan and interest rate locked in determine the amount paid each month, quarter, or year. Annuities can be great options for individuals who don't want to make investment decisions in retirement and need to know that they are receiving a set amount of annual income each year no matter what the markets and interest rates are doing. There are many advantages and disadvantages to annuities and the latter includes locking in for life at the currently low interest rates. Also, the calculations are based on life expectancy, so, because, statistically, women live longer a female investor would receive a lower annual payment over her life compared to an annuity for her male counterpart (all else remaining equal). Life annuities are purchased through insurance companies and fixed annuities can be purchased through many financial institutions. For more in-depth material on annuities, please visit my website at www.kelleykeehn.com/themoneybook.html

Recap

- RRSPs are a great investment option for many Canadians, but not for everyone and every situation. An RRSP might not be the ideal investment choice for those needing funds before retirement, in a low tax bracket, or with large pensions or income considerations at retirement.

- Tax-free savings accounts are a terrific investment vehicle for those for whom an RRSP isn't ideal or for those who have maxed out their RRSP contributions for the year, want to make a purchase in the short- to mid-term, or use a savings tool that isn't taxed as it grows.

- The essential difference between a registered investment and a non-registered investment is simply the tax implications of each. One shelter allows the investments to grow tax deferred; without a shelter, tax is due each year or at the sale of the investment. Plus, an RRSP produces a tax deduction.

- An RRSP must be converted to a RRIF or annuity at age 71 and income must then be withdrawn based on the RRIF tables. Any withdrawals of a RRSP or RRIF are taxable as income. With an RRSP, withholding tax would also apply should a withdrawal be made.

- RRSPs and RRIFs can be rolled over to a spouse at death, but in the absence of a spouse (or choice not to roll over to a spouse), the RRSP or RRIF becomes fully taxable (at the marginal tax rate of the holder the year of death).

For a complete list of definitions and illustrations further explaining the concepts in this chapter, please visit www.kelleykeehn.com/themoneybook.html.

Chapter 6

Debt

Quick Quiz

1. If interest rates are low and starting to rise, the economy is expected to:

A. Soften as people become afraid to make purchases as interest rates start to increase (major purchases such as homes and cars)

B. The economy always heats up as interest rates are rising

C. I have no idea; why would I care to follow where interest rates are going?

2. Your credit score is the only thing that matters when applying for a mortgage:

True ☐
False ☐

3. You can negotiate the rate of your mortgage with your prospective lender.

True ☐
False ☐

4. Once you've decided on an amortization, there's nothing you can do to reduce it.

True ☐
False ☐

5. In the long-term, a variable rate mortgage will generally cost less than a comparable fixed rate mortgage over, say, a 25-year amortization.

True ☐
False ☐

Debt should be a four-letter word in our society. Scrutinizing your debt in many ways is more important than focusing on your investments, especially in your early years. Unless you're investing in a fixed-rate GIC or lower risk bond, your rate of return is unknown. And, with guaranteed investments in today's marketplace, the interest rates are historically low (2.3% for a five-year non-redeemable GIC as of November 2010, for example). So, unless there were a double-digit investment on the market that would guarantee your principal and interest (and there isn't), it's best to focus on your debt, which will almost always have an interest rate higher than current guaranteed rates. Sure, if you invest in the stock market or an equity mutual fund, you may have a double-digit year here and there when you make more than you owe; however, it won't be consistent. Paying down high-interest debt (and sometimes any debt) before thinking of investing is prudent.

Today's interest rate environment favours new home buyers since current mortgage rates are at historical lows. I remember when I was starting the CFP (Certified Financial Planning) program back in 1994. Our instructor told us that if we could help our clients pay no more than 10% interest over their mortgage lifetime, we were doing a good job. Today, I think many people would have to walk away from their homes if mortgage rates increased to double digits. And there are many more homeowners out there who remember rates over 20% in the '80s.

When it comes to credit cards and loans, however, those rates haven't decreased much, if at all, since rates plummeted. Many credit cards still charge 19–29% interest, not to mention other fees and charges that you need to pay attention to. Reducing balances, knowing your rights as a borrower, and learning strategies for reducing debt is as important, perhaps even more important, than your investments (until you're debt free that is).

Interest Rates

Interest rates tell us a great deal about what's happening in the economy and what could happen in the future. When rates are low, consumers feel more prosperous and will generally consider spending more if their jobs are secure (among other factors). If rates are low when it's time to purchase a home, you'll be able to get into a bigger home, have a smaller mortgage payment, or need a smaller down payment than if rates are high. Since a home is likely to be your largest purchase in your lifetime, knowing which direction interest rates will go is extremely important, even though it is impossible to guarantee accuracy.

I've purchased two homes in my lifetime and have guessed wrong on interest rates both times. As a seasoned financial professional, I knew to research and carefully examine the economic indicators that drive rates—I still guessed wrong. A general rule that sometimes works (but don't stake your house on it) is that the bank usually offers consumers what is in the bank's best interest, not yours. For example, if a bank feels that long-term interest rates are going to rise in the future, they don't want consumers to lock in to a mortgage that is five years or longer. Think of it like this: if today's five-year mortgage rate is 7% and the bank thinks that in two or three years the rate will be 10%, it's in their best interest to deter you from locking in because if you did you would enjoy a few years at a rate lower than the market rate. Like all of us, banks don't have crystal balls and aren't always correct, but they generally know more than the average consumer about which direction rates are heading.

In today's lending environment, secured lines of credit (SLOC) and equity takeouts are all the rage. For a number of years, banks have been promoting the option of a SLOC as opposed to a conventional mortgage. This offers maximum flexibility because the borrower can pay off their SLOC any time without penalty, can use the "room" again just like a credit card, and receives a rate of interest at the prime rate or slightly below prime. Prime is the rate set by financial institutions based on the cost of short-term funds and on competitive pressures. The interest rate fluctuates with the prime rate; it increases or decreases along with it.

A conventional mortgage works similar to a GIC, but in reverse. The bank is the lender and you are the borrower. You choose the term, usually six months to seven years, and some banks now even have ten-year terms. The term is the amount of time that your interest rate is locked in, for better or worse, and the time period that you are locked in with that lender. The amortization of a mortgage is a bit trickier to understand. The amortization can be up to twenty-five years and, with some banks, thirty years. The longer the amortization schedule used, the lower your payments. If you pick a shorter amortization, your payments will be larger, but you'll also pay your principal off quicker and pay less interest in the long run. The amortization is simply a schedule used by the bank to determine your mortgage payment.

Let's use the example of a 25-year amortization on a five-year fixed rate mortgage of 7%. You would be locked in to that bank with a mortgage term of five years. If rates declined in that five-year term, you would lose out. If they increased during that time, you would benefit.

The 25-year amortization is only an estimate of what your payment would be if you took 25 years to pay off your mortgage, and if your rate remained constant over that time period. You are not locked in for 25 years; it's simply a schedule. When your term expires at your bank, you can renegotiate your mortgage or even move it to another financial institution. You can then recalculate your amortization and shorten or lengthen it depending on how quickly you'd like to pay the mortgage off.

Using Lending Products

STUDENT LOANS

In 2005 Statistics Canada indicated that the average Canadian bachelor's degree student graduates with a $18,000 debt. This number continues to rise. Graduates do see the return of their investment in the workforce, however, learning to manage student debt and pay it off as quickly as possible is necessary to ensure a more secure financial future.

Some facts about Canadian/provincial student loans—Although student loans give you a six-month grace period to beginning paying down the loan, interest on the loans starts to accumulate *the day you graduate*. The interest is on the total amount of the loan and the truth remains, it is best to pay it off as soon as possible. Refusal to make payments will be reported to credit bureaus and can have significant penalties.

One of the best pieces of advice I have heard is to keep living like a student after graduating. Try to keep your costs minimal. Although receiving that first paycheque is so exciting, the quicker you can get rid of your student debt the more money you will save. Remember to save all your student receipts and information: depending on your income you can carry over tax credits for that hard-earned education.

BANK LOANS

Consumers seek bank loans for a variety of reasons. It might be for a car or to renovate a home. A loan has a term over which you must pay back the principal borrowed along with interest. Some loans may be paid off early, with or without penalty. The bank may or may not require collateral depending on your security of employment, level of income, and creditworthiness. Collateral is some asset of value that a lender might require for security against your loan. In the case of a mortgage, the collateral is your house, but in the case of a loan, it could be your car, cash assets secured against your loan, or other such assets. Collateral assignments might be necessary for granting a loan and might even be required by the lender. In cases where the lender doesn't require security (e.g., an unsecured line of credit), the borrower may still choose to back their loan with collateral that will reduce the interest rate resulting from the bank being fully protected.

CREDIT CARDS

A wide range of financial institutions in Canada issue credit cards. They offer the holder an amount of credit that can be used for purchases. The entire balance can be paid off each month without penalty or just a minimum amount each month (usually 3% of the outstanding balance). Credit cards have extremely wide variances for the interest rate charged for unpaid balances, which can range from 10% to nearly 29%. That doesn't include other charges such as annual fees or penalties for being over an established credit limit.

Credit cards are a useful tool to the disciplined holder. A major benefit to making purchases on a credit card is that it can act like a purchases monitor, keeping all expenses in one handy consolidated statement each month. Another valuable feature, which can be found on many gold or platinum cards, is a reward-point system that can be applied to anything from flights to various purchases. Other benefits included in some premium cards are travel protection, theft/loss protection, and much more. However, many consumers don't take the time to learn about these benefits and, if they are not used, the cost of the annual fee could easily outweigh their value. Always check the fine print and know the interest rate, fees, and entitlements of your card.

A credit card (and other debt) is also called a demand loan and for good reason; the issuer/lender can demand the entire balance be paid in full at any time. Most Canadians never give this much thought, but during the height of the recent crash in the US (mid-2009) many US credit companies reduced the maximums on clients' accounts or closed their accounts and demanded full payment. As mentioned earlier, according to CNBC, at the time 62% of credit card holders were facing some sort of squeeze.

Years ago a girlfriend of mine received an extremely threatening surprise call from a creditor. The caller was demanding that she pay her balance and interest on her credit card account that day. She didn't even know what the rude collector was talking about. The credit card in question was an old Holt Renfrew department store card. She knew she was close to the maximum, but she had always paid her minimum monthly payment. Stunned, she listened to the caller. What had happened was American Express had bought out all of the Holt Renfrew card accounts. Because her credit wasn't stellar, AMEX did not approve her and wouldn't roll her balance over. As a result her account was due in full. The caller phoned her a day before a letter stating the same arrived (never settle anything on the phone with anyone unless you have something in writing). She had no choice but to borrow the funds from family to pay the almost $5,000 debt.

UNSECURED LINES OF CREDIT (USLOC)

A USLOC is similar to a credit card in that your limit and use is revolving (you can run it up to the maximum, pay it down or off, etc.). The difference is that you may or may not have an actual card attached to the USLOC. Maximum amounts are usually much greater than those of credit cards, but not always.

A USLOC is not secured by a home or asset. The lender approves the USLOC on the borrower's creditworthiness, employment security, and servicing ability, amongst other criteria.

Buying a Home

As discussed previously, a mortgage, in its simplest terms, is a more structured loan requiring a chattel against a home. The lender now has an interest in your home and will register that legally binding interest. They will be listed on your land title. Most banks will not lend funds or provide a mortgage for undeveloped land.

A mortgage has a set interest rate for a given term (six months to seven years depending on the financial institution). Payments consist of principal repayment and interest. During the early years of a mortgage, the majority of the payments go towards interest. During the later years, most of your dollars are paying off the principal. Most mortgages allow you to increase your payment (so you can pay your mortgage off quicker) and also allow you to make an annual or semi-annual lump sum payment (that is applied directly to the principal) without penalty. This payment is usually capped to a maximum of 10 to 20%.

Should you have an unexpected windfall and have the available cash to fully pay off your mortgage before its term, you will pay a penalty to the bank called the interest differential. The bank will calculate this amount for you upon request. Should interest rates fall dramatically from the time you lock in your mortgage rate, paying the penalty could be more advantageous than staying in at a higher rate.

Lenders and the mortgage terms they offer are more flexible today than ever and most have options that will allow you to pay off your mortgage sooner, decrease the length of your amortization, and make extra payments as set forth by your agreement. These extra payments are penalty free and can add up to substantial savings since they are applied directly to the principal. If you are unaware of your options, check your mortgage document or call up your lender. Conversely, individuals who are stretched with their mortgage payment or would like to own a more expensive home sooner, can opt for the longest amortization period available to get the lowest payment possible. This group can still benefit throughout the term by paying down on principal during anniversaries or by increasing monthly payments where permitted.

Most financial institutions encourage consumers to make their payments bi-monthly as opposed to monthly to pay off the mortgage more quickly. (With a bi-monthly schedule, you'll actually make one extra payment per year.) Depending on when you receive your paycheque or other regular income payments, you may wish to structure your payments to coincide with your cash flow.

In Canada, you need to put down 20% of the home's appraised value to avoid CMHC (Canadian Mortgage and Housing Corporation) insurance fees. CMHC is a crown corporation and insures the bank's interest in case the mortgage holder defaults. The thinking behind these mortgage guidelines is that if you have at least 20% invested in their home, you're unlikely to walk away. To clarify what I'm talking about, let's imagine that someone had a home worth $300,000 when they purchased it, but today its value has gone down to $250,000. Let's assume they only put 5% down when they bought it, so the mortgage on the property would still be around $285,000 making the home "upside down": there is more owing on the house than it's worth. We recently saw a lot of homeowners who were upside down at the height of the US housing crisis and we continue to hear reports in the media. Unfortunately, when this happens, some owners simply walk away and leave the lender on the hook.

In the most simple of terms, a mortgage is comprised of three main parts and thus, you have three major decisions to make once you've shopped around for choice of products and negotiated the interest rate:

- The down payment
- Your term
- The amortization

The down payment

In Canada, as mentioned, to qualify as a conventional mortgage that's not subject to CMHC fees, you need a down payment of at least 20% of the home's purchase price. Depending on other factors, such as your credit and employment, you may need more or less as a down payment to get approved for a mortgage. For now, let's look at the difference between down payments and the cost or savings of the insurance.

	Option 1	Option 2	Option 3	Option 4
Purchase Price	$180,832	$192,282	$220,644	$226,515
Down Payment Amount	$9,042	$19,228	$44,129	$50,000
Down Payment	5%	10%	20%	22.1%
Mortgage Principal Amount	$171,791	$173,054	$176,515	$176,515
Default Insurance Premium	$4,724	$3,461	$0	$0
Total Mortgage Amount	$176,515	$176,515	$176,515	$176,515
Payment Amount	$932	$932	$932	$932

Source: Numbers calculated using RBC's "How Much Can I Afford?" tool, found at

www.rbcroyalbank.com/cgi-bin/mortgage/tools/howmuch/afford.pl

As you can see, with option three or four, you wouldn't be subject to CMHC insurance. Before you decide to buy, you'll want to factor in the cost of the insurance as opposed to saving up for a larger down payment or purchasing a less expensive home. As you can see from the chart, if you do choose to take advantage of home ownership with less than 20% as a down payment, make sure you discuss all of the options that come into play with having an insured mortgage. For instance, the insurance premium you'll pay depends on how much of a down payment you come in with (i.e., the premium is higher for 5% down than 10%), if you're self-employed, if you'd like the option of taking your mortgage with you to another home (called portability), and more. You might also note that the payments in the chart are all the same, however, the lower the down payment, the lower the cost of the home will have to be to keep the payment consistent.

To illustrate the difference in payment frequency, the following chart was based on the "total mortgage amount" used in the previous chart of $176,515, a 25-year amortization, and a fixed five-year rate of 4.04%:

Payment Frequency	Amount	Amortization	Total Interest Cost	Savings vs. Monthly Payment
Monthly	$932	25.0 years	$103,185	$0
Semi-Monthly	$466	25.0 years	$102,785	$400
Bi-Weekly	$430	24.9 years	$102,066	$1,119
Weekly	$215	24.9 years	$101,883	$1,302
Accelerated Bi-Weekly	$466	21.8 years	$87,956	$15,229
Accelerated Weekly	$233	21.8 years	$87,791	$15,394

Source: Calculated using RBC's "Mortgage Payment Calculator"

www.rbcroyalbank.com/products/mortgages/mortgage_calculators.html

You can see how paying weekly can reduce your amortization and of course, save you considerable interest. With bi-weekly payments, you're essentially making an extra payment each year as opposed to the other options.

Your term

This seems to be the great debate in mortgages today: Is a fixed-term or a variable rate mortgage better? Which one is best for you and your family?

I'll explain the amortization shortly, but for now think of it as an estimate of the time you'll take to pay your entire mortgage. The amortization is generally between 15 and 25 years (but you can go higher or lower).

The term relates to the agreed upon length of time you'll pay an interest rate and if that rate is fixed or if it floats with the prime rate. Of course, the bank won't lock your interest rate in for a decade or more, so you have a wide variety of term options. You can have a closed term, which will gives you a lower rate of interest than an open. With a closed term, say five years, you're locked in to that interest rate with that bank, for five years. You would have to pay a penalty to the bank if you wanted to pay off your mortgage entirely (say you inherited some money or won the lotto), or if, for example, in year three rates are lower and you want a new term at a lower rate or you'd like to switch the mortgage to another bank before it matures. Makes sense—they're guaranteeing you a rate for a set time and if you find something better or your life changes, unfortunately, you'd have a pay a penalty for getting out of the agreement. In the case where interest rates dropped during your term, some banks and mortgages will allow the option of a blended rate—they'll allow you to split the difference between your current rate and the new, lower rate.

With an open mortgage, you'll pay a higher rate of interest, however, if you're uncertain about rates or your situation in the near future, it might be a better option as you wouldn't face a penalty if you decided to pay it off, switch lenders, etc. But this option isn't ideal for most mortgage holders.

Take a look at these closed fixed term rates from RBC. As of December 1, 2010, the open and closed fixed term rates were:

Term	Posted Rate	Special Offers
1 Year	3.350%	2.950%
2 Year	3.600%	
3 Year	4.150%	
4 Year	4.940%	4.040%
5 Year	5.190%	4.040%
7 Year	6.350%	4.800%
10 Year	6.500%	4.950%
25 Year	8.250%	
Open		
6 month	6.300%	
1 year	6.300%	

Source: RBC

I chose RBC as an example; however, BMO, Scotia, TD, and CIBC all had very similar, if not identical, rates. Some banks don't offer a term longer than seven years and every bank has its own unique enticements and special products. I'll discuss shopping around shortly. You'll see in the list of rates a column called "special offers." Years ago, before the popularity of the internet, you'd have to call around to different banks or visit them in person to find out their respective rates. Then, you'd have to be a pretty shrewd negotiator to get that rate down by a quarter or half a percent. Today, because "posted rates" are so easy to locate on each bank's website, they all also offer special deals (in addition to what you might be able to further negotiate). The "posted rate" is just the un-discounted rate. All of this information at your fingertips is so important because you can shop around just about as easily as a mortgage broker can (with the main big six banks in Canada any-way – not the subprime and alternative lenders) when just a decade or so ago, this shopping process would have been too arduous for most mortgage seekers.

There's another, very popular choice called a variable rate term. This rate floats with prime and you can still have an open or closed term. The difference is that your interest rate isn't fixed.

As of December 1, 2010, the open and closed variable rates with RBC were:

Variable Rate Mortgages

Term	Posted Rate
Closed	
5 year	Prime Rate - 0.150%
Open	
5 year	Prime Rate + 0.700%

Source: RBC's "Variable Rate Mortgages"
www.rbcroyalbank.com/products/mortgages/view_rates.html

The prime rate at the time was 3%, so for a closed, five-year variable mortgage, the rate would be 2.85% and for a five-year open, it would be 3.7%.

As you can see from the charts above, using the example of a closed, five-year variable rate of 2.85% and that of a closed five-year fixed rate term of 4.04%, there's a difference of 1.19%. That seemingly small difference could save you thousands of dollars over the term of your mortgage. However, if rates increase, it could cost significantly if you decided to lock into a fixed rate later.

So, back to the fixed vs. variable debate. Which one is better? Let's consider a few things. First, one would need to have a crystal ball to know where interests rates are going—even the "experts" can't predict this. No one knows for sure, but the fact is that rates, as I write this, are at a historic low. If they will increase much and when it will happen would be yet another guess. Second, historically, a variable rate, over the long term, will be lower in comparison to a fixed rate. The problem with a historical argument is that it doesn't factor in the rates today and what will happen tomorrow. The third is what I call the "tummy factor." What can you handle? Will you watch rates? Do you have a propensity for risk when it comes to the rate of your mortgage or would you prefer to lock-in at a very low and reasonable rate and forget it for five years? Either is a little bit of a gamble—the latter less so.

Banks have become more and more creative with mortgage options over the years and many offer products that capitalize on both the fixed and variable options. Some allow you a portion of your mortgage to be locked in with a secured line of credit as part of it (with a variable rate). Some offer variable rate mortgages with the option of locking in if rates increase.

Generally speaking, a variable rate mortgage works for someone who is willing to take a little risk. Consider that if rates do increase and your mortgage allows you to lock in at a new fixed rate, it won't be the fixed rate of today. Make sure you examine the numbers, but also your comfort level when it comes to choosing a rate.

The amortization

The third main element of a mortgage is your choice of amortization. As mentioned, this is the estimated length of time it will take you to pay off your mortgage based on your interest rate at the time of signing, the term (assuming rates stayed the same for the years you chose, which of course they won't), and the monthly payment. The longer your amortization, the lower your payment and the shorter, the higher. Again, it's simply an estimate and with many options, such as weekly or bi-weekly payments, increasing your monthly payments, or making annual payments (the extra goes directly to paying off your principal amount) you can reduce your amortization. Amortization, therefore, is simply an estimate at the time of signing of when you'll pay off your mortgage.

Let's take a look at a $250,000 mortgage at today's five-year fixed rate of 4.04% and what different amortizations would look like, the monthly payments, and the total interest paid over the life of the mortgage (again, assuming everything remains constant). Remember that paying more frequently on your mortgage will reduce the amortization and interest costs, but for this example, I'm using a monthly payment for each for consistency.

15-year amortization:
- Monthly payment = $1,850.03
- Term interest costs = $43,673.46 (over the five-year period)
- Amortization interest costs = $83,003.68 (over 15 years)

20-year amortization:
- Monthly payment = $1,515.80
- Term interest costs = $45,782.37 (over the five-year period)
- Amortization interest costs = $113,790.32 (over 20 years)

You can see that with a longer amortization, 20 years as opposed to 15, you'd pay about $334 less per month for your payment, but you'd pay just about $31,000 more in interest over the amortization in exchange for the lower monthly payment. Let's look at the same mortgage, this time with a 35-year amortization.

35-year amortization:

- Monthly payment = $1,107.90
- Term interest costs = $48,356.11 (over the five-year period)
- Amortization interest costs = $215,316.48 (over 35 years)

This third example of a 35-year mortgage is much more extreme. With this option over the 15-year amortization, your monthly payment would be about $742 less, but you'd pay a whopping $132,312 over the total life of the mortgage. Why? First, because of the lower payment, and second because you'd be paying for 20 years longer. The magic of compound interest, but in the bank's favour. Not only do rates change, but so does the government's view on banking regulation. As of January 2011, the government is proposing several changes to the mortgage rules and one is to reduce the maximum amortization allowed from 35 to 30 years. Remember to visit my site at www.kelleykeehn.com/themoneybook. html for updated information about this.

So which amortization term should you chose?

The longest amortization will allow a first time homeowner to get into a large house or simply keep their payment lower. This could be a great lifestyle choice, however, one needs to keep the total interest to be paid in mind and possibly chose a home that costs less. Most experts agree, and perhaps you do as well, that more and more Canadians are getting into homes they can narrowly afford and many complain about being house poor. Don't just look at the monthly payment when deciding on a home and mortgage. Ensure that you pay attention to how long you'll have that mortgage and be fully aware of the interest that you'll pay over the life of it. Hopefully the latter will deter you from purchasing too soon or beyond your budget. Plus, with Canadian interest rates still at a nearly all-time low, you can expect that the estimated interest you'll pay over the life of your mortgage is likely to be higher than what you

calculate at today's rates.

But if cash flow is tight in the early years or one wanted to create a cushion for emergencies, remember that the amortization can be reduced over the years by paying more frequently (bi-weekly), increasing monthly payments, and making annual lump sum payments to principal. See my mortgage burning story later in this chapter for an illustration.

SECURED LINES OF CREDIT (SLOC)

Like a mortgage, a SLOC is secured against your home via a chattel, but unlike a mortgage, it offers the consumer flexibility. Let's assume that you purchased a home for $350,000 by putting $100,000 down and choosing a SLOC for $250,000 to pay the rest. Think of this amount, or credit limit, like a credit card—just without the card. As you pay down the $250,000, you're free to run the amount up again, which, depending on your discipline, could be a good or bad thing. A SLOC also provides some contingency planning, as you only need to pay the interest costs per month. This makes your required monthly payment less than that of a mortgage, which forces you to pay down the principal as well. For example, with an equal amount borrowed, a mortgage payment might be $1,200 per month (interest and principal) whereas a SLOC may require an interest-only payment of $700 per month. By paying only the interest on the SLOC, the balance would never be paid down. This is not an option with a regular mortgage. However, in a month of financial crisis, having an interest-only low-minimum-payment option as a temporary fail-safe could be a feature you'd appreciate. The major problem with this option is that many Canadians don't have the discipline to pay more than the interest (that's all that's required monthly) and after many years, they might find they haven't paid a penny in principal.

Remember that a SLOC's rate fluctuates with the prime lending rate of Canada, so if it's important for you to have a set monthly mortgage bill for five to seven years, opt for a conventional mortgage.

EQUITY TAKEOUTS

An equity takeout simply means that your home has either risen in value or you have paid down your mortgage enough to build up excess equity in your home. Assuming a conventional mortgage, let's estimate that with the mortgage payments you've made and a recent increase in the value of your house, your mortgage is now only 62% of the appraised value. With equity takeout, the financial institution may rewrite your mortgage or offer other options to use the 18% equity in your home (assuming you had a conventional mortgage and maintain 20% equity).

Since a mortgage is the largest liability most of us will have in a lifetime, I'd like to go in-depth on this particular debt. Let's look at how best to negotiate it and strategies for paying it down, as well as understanding and living with it. A mortgage is not a document that should just be filed and only looked at when renewing, it should be thought about at least quarterly and examined in-depth at least once of year. Every quarter you should crunch the numbers to determine how many years you could knock off your mortgage if you allocated just a few extra dollars a day to your principal. Once a year you want to look at rates—are you in a variable and are rates ready to rise? Or, are you in a fixed term and rates have dropped dramatically? Might your banker be able to offer you a better blended rate or would breaking your mortgage, paying the penalty and locking in for a new fixed term make sense?

Burn Your Mortgage

During the spring and summer of 2010, I was the financial host of a reality TV series called *Burn My Mortgage* that aired on the W Network. We shot thirteen episodes with thirteen families and focused specifically on how each family could be mortgage free sooner—think *The Amazing Race* meets home finance. By the end of the season, even I was shocked by the numbers.

We took the families through three financial challenges per episode to show them first where they were spending their money (most truly had no idea) and second how many years they'd burn off of their mortgages and how many thousands of dollars they could save if they reduced their spending (not eliminate it), and applied their savings to their mortgage principal annually. The show was about choice and awareness, not sacrifice, so we never asked families to eradicate their budgets, just tweak them in the name of mortgage freedom.

Remember my story about compound interest in Chapter 3? It works in reverse with a mortgage, especially if you have a long amortization. If you currently have or have had a mortgage and opened your annual statement, you'd see that in the beginning years, you're paying mostly interest. However, as you are now well aware, most Canadian mortgages (check your document), allow holders to make annual payments, increase monthly payments, and more. Sadly, too many Canadians opt for the "skip a payment" option each year rather than taking the opportunity to pay down the mortgage quicker.

Until I was involved in *Burn My Mortgage*, perhaps because of my age and because my financial career was investment not debt focused, I had never heard of a mortgage burning party. Apparently they existed, although they're pretty much a thing of the past. In today's "bigger is better" homeowner environment, even empty nesters are not downsizing as they did in the past, so fewer people are getting rid of their mortgages entirely.

If you're wondering how much a few cuts here and there can affect a mortgage, let's take a look at Dale and Todd's situation from *Burn My Mortgage*, Episode 10.

Dale and Todd
Married with two teenage boys
Mortgage amount: $225,000
Interest rate: 4.2%
Amortization: 30 years*
Interest costs: $190,000*
Actual cost of their mortgage: $445,000
*assuming the rates remained constant over the 30-year period

Dale and Todd, and really every family on the show were, at first look, doing everything right. They didn't have any credit card debt and paid their mortgage on time each and every month. The common theme with all 13 families was:

- Most of them knew they could pay extra on their mortgage principal each month but didn't feel they had enough money left at the end of the month to do so.

- Most were shocked when we added up what they were spending their money on each month. Even more jaw dropping was when I'd tell them how much they were looking at paying in interest over the life of their mortgage (all things remaining equal from when they originally signed their bank documents).

CHALLENGE #1: EATING OUT

Who isn't guilty of occasionally turning to take-out or going out to eat as a way to remove some stress from hectic family life? But to the tune of $600 a month or $7,200 a year? That's what Dale and Todd's family were spending and they had no idea the number was that extreme. We actually had one family who spent $1,000 a month on eating out. Before we let them in on the number and asked them how much they thought they were spending, they replied, "Oh, it's likely a few hundred dollars." That's a big difference.

The challenge was to involve Mom, Dad, and the boys in a grocery store challenge to see how much food they could buy, then to cook a breakfast at home together the next morning. They then compared their receipt to the money they would have used eating out, like they did most weekends.

We only asked them to reduce their eating out by half (we wouldn't expect anyone to cut it out entirely). Doing this would free up $300 a month or $3,600 a year that they could be apply to their mortgage principal annually.

If they did that, they would burn nine years off of their mortgage and save $67,000 in interest! Even I found that number shocking.

Challenge #2: The newest and best gizmos

This was an electronics-focused family with the latest and greatest of everything. We asked them to get creative and seek out last year's models of MP3 players, TVs, computers, and more. To illustrate their old "junk," and how much they've spent over the years, we took them to a massive electronics recycling graveyard where all these gadgets go to die.

We asked them to cut their $6,000 a year electronics spending in half. If they added that $250 a month to the first challenge, they'd have $550 a month, or $6,600 a year to apply to their mortgage principal annually.

And, if they did that, they'd burn 14 years off their mortgage and save $95,000 in interest.

CHALLENGE #3: PRIORITIZE ACTIVITIES

We weren't done yet. This family was spending upwards of $2,000 a month on recreational activities and equipment. The boys were involved in just about every sport you can imagine! With this challenge, the boys even chimed in that there were a lot of sports and activities that they weren't even interested in. It was easy, as a family, to prioritize the ones the boys wanted to keep the most.

We didn't even ask the family to cut down by half. Actually, we simply asked them to reduce their spending by $500 a month. If they did that and added it to the savings from the first two challenges, they'd have a total of $1,050 a month or $12,600 annually to put down on their mortgage principal.

And the grand finale result? They'd burn 18 years off of their mortgage and save $125,000 in interest over the life of their mortgage. It was an eye opener and even jaw dropper when we announced it at the end of shooting.

Simply being aware, prioritizing spending, and allocating the savings to their mortgage principal would have Dale and Todd mortgage free in 12 years as opposed to 30. That's a huge difference in lifestyle! The course that Dale and Todd were on saw them retiring with little to no savings, the kids taking on debt for university, and working longer to pay off the mortgage. A little creative reduction here and there will allow Dale and Todd to be mortgage free in time to assist the boys with their education and save for their retirement.

MORTGAGE PSYCHOLOGY 101

For many of the families on *Burn My Mortgage*, because they were spending money and not saving it, opening their eyes to the impact of paying down their mortgage quicker was a sort of forced savings plan. Our long-term hope for many of these families is that once they've paid off their largest debt and have developed more astute spending patterns, they'll actually be able to save for their retirement as well.

MY TOP TIPS FOR BURNING YOUR MORTGAGE

1. *Negotiate—yes you can!* The posted rates are rarely the actual rates you can get by simply asking. Consider that on a $250,000 mortgage, a 1% difference could save you $43,841.29 during the life of your mortgage (based on a five-year fixed, paid bi-weekly, a 25 year amortization and the difference between a steady 5% vs. 4% interest rate).

2. *Learn the basics.* If you're not a financial wiz—no worries. Read the previous sections about amortization, fixed, and variable terms. Be sure to check out your bank's website talking to your banker—they likely have a list of definitions, useful articles, and calculators.

3. *Buy now or later?* Remember all the costs involved in home ownership. You shouldn't spend more than 32% of your gross income on housing expenses. And don't forget property taxes, insurance, closing costs, condo fees, and more!

4. *Hold the rate!* If you're not quite ready to buy, call your banker. They'll often hold the current interest rate for 90–180 days.

5. *Fixed vs. variable.* Experts say that over the life of a mortgage, a variable rate will generally win. However, with rates at an all-time low (as of January 2011) and likely ready to climb, you need to know your interest rate risk factor. If rates climbed even a couple of percentage points, your mortgage payment could nearly double. Could you handle an increase?

6. *The best of both worlds.* Many banks today offer a combination of a fixed rate mortgage with a portion set up as a line of credit that floats with prime.

7. *RRSP vs. paying down the mortgage—what's the best bet?* What about doing both! If you're a high-income earner, an RRSP is hard to beat. But ensure you take the tax refund and apply it directly to your mortgage principal. Not only will you be saving for your retirement while taking advantage of a great tax break, but you could also save thousands of dollars on your mortgage and shave years off its length.

8. *Buy now or wait?* If you don't have at least 20% for a down payment, you will have to purchase CMHC insurance. Depending on the size of your mortgage, this could cost you thousands of dollars. Do some calculations and ask your banker if it's best to save up a little longer.

9. *Do it more often.* Paying bi-weekly or better yet, weekly, makes an extra payment a year that can add up to big bucks!

10. *To insure or not to insure?* Mortgage insurance is generally a pretty good idea and your bank may require it. The question is, should you purchase the insurance they offer or shop around for a private policy? The latter could be less costly and you have absolute control of who gets the amount at your death.

MORTGAGE BROKER OR DO-IT-YOURSELF?

The lending landscape has changed dramatically over the last decade in Canada and the US. We have more small, non-bank type lenders opening up on every street corner in every major city. We only need to open a newspaper today to read about the bankruptcies and foreclosures of our friends to the south.

When the big banks say no to a mortgage request, you really need to reflect on why. Be extremely cautious when your desire to own a home supersedes the common sense of what you can truly afford. If your monthly payments are too big for you, you risk fore-closure.

Mortgage brokers are men and women who I believe are offering what they feel are valuable products and services—and many are. But before you decide if you need a broker, let's look at a few criticisms of the industry.

Our desire in this century to have now what would have taken our parents and grandparents a lifetime to acquire has led to financial troubles for many. Home ownership, for example, is a very worthy goal and one all Canadians should strive for. However, with many owners seeking a bigger house, smaller down payments, and barely being approved for a mortgage, the situation of being house poor is rampant and quite frankly, not a great deal of fun. For many, renting and saving up for a few more years could provide the cushion that makes home ownership more comfortable in the long term.

Once fairly rare, the use of brokers has become a lot more common, especially among younger, first-time buyers. While mortgage brokers are responsible for about 30% of the mortgage business in Canada, a CMHC survey from early 2009 showed that 44% of first-time buyers used mortgage brokers in 2009. Compare that to 35% in 2007.

There are basically two main reasons a seeker of debt (usually a mortgage) would use a broker:

1. Brokers will shop the best rates.
2. Many brokers have access to alternative lenders you might not be aware of.

First, it is true that a broker will contact a number of banks and lenders on your behalf. This is a valid reason for using a broker because if you were to seek approval from a number of lenders yourself in a short period of time, this could greatly reduce your credit score (see my explanation of this in Chapter 1). However, what a broker won't tell you is that you can shop around yourself. Simply purchase your current credit report, bring it into an initial interview with your lender and discuss the likelihood of your approval, interest rate, and terms. Be upfront with them that you're shopping around and not consenting for them to pull your credit report. If you do choose to move forward with that lender, they will eventually need to pull your report, however, they'll have been able to give you a good estimate about the probability of your approval. If you were unlikely to be approved, there would be no sense in getting them to put a direct hit on your report and reduce your score further.

My second argument against using a broker is that if a major bank, which usually has the more stringent lending criteria, won't approve your mortgage, is it still in your best interest to seek one out? If you said yes, then this is where a broker will come to the table, but usually for a significant fee.

I've personally met a number of caring and helpful brokers who simply wanted to help their clients get into a home quicker when it seemed nearly impossible or less likely that they would be able to secure a mortgage through a standard lender. However, you have to ask yourself the question, at what cost?

Always (I can't stress this enough) ask for the fine print in advance. No one works for free and nor should they, however, before signing on the dotted line and before anyone pulls your credit report, ensure that you've seen and read the fine print regarding fees, interest rates, hidden administration costs, and more. Too often, by the time someone is faced with signing the papers, they might feel it's too late to back out. This is especially true with subprime mortgages, which are riskier to the lender. Subprime mortgages are sought by homeowners with impaired credit, unstable or inconsistent income. Their interest rates are higher (sometimes quite a bit higher along with other fees) than what would be paid with the big six banks or a prime lender. A subprime lender can be found with a mortgage broker and more and more have moved up here from the US (such as CitiFinancial and WellsFargo, although many closed their Canadian doors after the crisis hit in the US). Whatever the financial choices you make, just be sure to know the risks and rewards.

Search the internet before you call your banker and be armed with the best rates on the market. Remember, like everything else in your financial life, your mortgage is negotiable. Just asking for a simple rate reduction from your bank can save you thousands of dollars.

Also don't feel you have to use the mortgage broker recommended by your real estate agent. If you do opt for a mortgage broker, I'd suggest calling up a Certified Financial Planner for some referrals. Usually these pros have vetted a few and always shop around. Generally CFPs are not allowed to be paid referral fees, so they're likely to give an honest referral. Plus, they have no vested interest in getting the deal approved, while the real estate agent does.

Before you even apply for a mortgage, get the bottom line costs to you, their fee, hidden fees, the interest rate, and details if the deal will be with a subprime lender.

MORTGAGE BROKER ADVANTAGES

I recently shared my bias of favouring the do-it-yourself mortgage approach, with a financial planner I highly respect. He was my CFP instructor years ago and is extremely well respected in the industry. I explained to him that after spending quite a bit of time doing business in the US at the height of the real estate crash my bias deepened further. So many of the mortgage troubles south of the border were precipitated and exacerbated by unscrupulous mortgage brokers (and those seeking the mortgages too).

My friend and colleague disagreed strongly. He asked if there was a way he could guarantee saving me, for example, $2,000 a year for 25 years, would I be interested? Of course, I answered. He explained that that's what a reputable mortgage broker can do for a consumer shopping for a mortgage. Because of their ability to negotiate with a number of banks on behalf of their clients, mortgage brokers can save considerable interest on their clients' mortgages by negotiating lower interest rates.

My rebuttal was two-fold. First, as a consumer, you can negotiate with a bank yourself. By simply asking for a rate reduction (and many of them have already discounted their rates as posted online), your bank will often work to accommodate you if you're a desirable customer (as mentioned before, you have the great credit score, cash flow, down payment, etc.). Second, if an individual isn't credit worthy according to the big six banks in Canada, the mortgage broker will do whatever it takes to get that person into a mortgage, even if it's with a subprime lender charging a much higher interest rate and a large number of hidden fees.

My friend did agree that the latter happens and it's disappointing. However, my friend also pointed out that in his experience as a VP for a major Canadian bank, most individuals would rarely negotiate their interest rate with their banker. Canadians are a polite bunch and most don't feel comfortable negotiating unless on a Mexican vacation.

So, there you have two issues to consider when dealing or not dealing with a mortgage broker. If you're the negotiating type and would be comfortable with simply asking your banker for a better rate (and why not, they want your business) and you're willing to do some shopping around, then you likely don't need a broker. If you wouldn't ask or the entire process of getting your own credit report and negotiating on your own behalf sounds too complex or intimidating, then, by all means, consider using a broker. However, if a subprime mortgage is presented to you as an option, please be ultra-careful to read the fine print and be prudent in determining if you can really afford that home. If the big banks in Canada won't approve your request, there is usually a good reason: you can't truly afford it!

RRSP OR PAY DOWN THE MORTGAGE?

This is a question I receive often. Should I use a certain dollar amount to pay down my mortgage principal, or should I use the funds to invest in an RRSP and then use the tax refund to pay down my mortgage principal? The second option is a very valid strategy that works best for those in a higher tax bracket (thus a higher tax deduction). As stated in the tax shelters section, RRSPs aren't right for everyone, but if they are for your situation, this could be an option to consider.

Let's look at Steve and Lydia's situation. Steve is an impulse spender and thinks that any money they have to invest should be put down on their mortgage; he worries he'll just blow a tax refund. Plus, he's worried about mortgage rates going up. Lydia thinks it makes much more sense for them to put the $6,000 they have set aside each year into an RRSP and use the tax refund to pay down the mortgage.

Their numbers:
- Annual household income: $120,000 (mostly his)
- Mortgage amount: $375,000
- Interest on 5-year fixed rate: 3.5%
- Amortization period: 25 years

- Mortgage payments paid bi-weekly
- Savings of $6,000 a year for 15 years
- Live in Ontario (this affects their marginal tax bracket)

Although not every financial situation can be solved by simply looking at the numbers, in this case, the numbers make more sense for the couple to invest in an RRSP and use the tax refund to pay down on the mortgage principal. However, for someone who feels that they'll just blow their tax refund, we need to consider other forces that are also at play and the need for some homeowners to pay down their mortgage as a forced savings plan.

Without a crystal ball, no one can know with certainty where rates will go and when. Many people blow their tax refunds, but what they need to keep in mind that a "refund" is actually their money that the government is returning—without interest. It's not found money to be blown. If you are a person who can get their head around that concept and resist the urge to spend it foolishly, the RRSP investment, especially with Steve and Lydia's income, makes the most sense.

Here are the numbers: (For the sake of this particular question, everything remains the same in both scenarios: both account for them still making the mortgage payments, constant rates, etc.)

Scenario one: put $6,000 annually on their mortgage principal for 15 years (we have to assume rates remain constant in both examples). With this strategy, they'll reduce their amortization down to 18.3 years and will save $60,211.99 in interest.

Scenario two: put $6,000 into an RRSP and use the $2,784.60 tax refund to pay down their mortgage principal for 15 years.

Using a very conservative rate of return of 3.5% (the same as their mortgage) as an estimate, after 15 years their RRSP would equal $119,993.13. Applying the tax refund to their principal would add up to a savings of $32,277 and reduce their amortization down to 21.7 years. Both of those savings add up to $152,270.26. That's a difference of $92,058.27 if the couple were to follow scenario two as opposed to one. And, considering that a balanced RRSP with moderate risk should earn more than 3.5% over a 15-year period, this option looks even better.

I equally like the idea of Steve and Lydia building a nest egg while they pay off their mortgage so they don't find themselves house poor at retirement.

Steve and Lydia also need to examine their financial situation before making their plan. The factors for them to look at include their risk tolerance with both their mortgage and RRSP. Also they should consider if they both have pensions that would make investing in an RRSP a tax deterrent at retirement (because of the extra forced income from a RRIF). I suggested to Steve and Lydia that they invest in a fee-only financial planner who will assess their entire picture, along with their savings and spending tendencies.

I should remind you that RRSPs are taxable if Steve and Lydia want to access the funds, but, had they applied the money only to their mortgage, they wouldn't readily be able to access that either. A further calculation could be done based on paying the mortgage off sooner and then allocating all mortgage payments to savings or even adding in the option of the tax-free savings account. However, too many factors make scenario two the clear choice for this couple. Seek the advice of a financial professional to outline all possible options for your unique situation.

Reverse Mortgages

You've probably seen them; those commercials telling seniors that thanks to their paid-off home, they're sitting on a gold mine. Why you too could be frolicking on the beach and helping your grandkids with their education or simply buying what you want, when you want. These ads are promoting a product called reverse mortgages and while the commercials would have you think these are the best retirement plans out there, they come with big risks and lots of fine print to examine.

WHAT EXACTLY IS A REVERSE MORTGAGE?

- They're an option for homeowners over the age of 60.
- A senior is able to tap into the equity in their home, up to 40% of its value.
- The ads are targeted at people who have already paid off their homes (although you can still qualify if you have an existing mortgage).
- People taking out a reverse mortgage don't make any payments unless they sell or move. Repayment would also be required in case of death.
- The amount a person receives can be paid in a lump sum or even monthly or in annual installments.
- The company that most people know is CHIP, or Canadian Home Income Plan, but there's another firm that offers reverse mortgages, called Seniors Money.

You don't make a payment during the life of the reverse mortgage (unless you sell, move, or pass away), but interest is compounding during that time period. This is the lure of the reverse mortgage, but it needs to be fully comprehended by the senior that the longer the reverse mortgage is in place, the more it's depleting equity in their home.

Although most experts in the financial industry feel this is a last resort strategy, it might have appeal to cash-strapped retirees. If someone wants to stay in their home and simply doesn't have the monthly income to manage the bills, wants to renovate their home, or perhaps needs money for home care assistance, it could be an option worth considering. Especially if that senior doesn't have a family to inherit the property.

When I was researching this topic for CBC radio last year, I spoke with PJ Wade. She's the author of *Reverse Mortgages: Best Friend, Worst Enemy...Your Choice!* As an expert on the subject, she stressed that education is key. She points out that many seniors do not realize that, while a reverse mortgage might end up being the right choice for them, there are other options they should consider first. She suggested that seniors start by looking five years into the future. Five years before they think they might need to tap into the value of their home, seniors should gather all available information regarding the options open to them—everything from reverse mortgages to home equity loans. This way if someone tries to sell them a product like a reverse mortgage down the road or they are suddenly in desperate need, they'll be well prepared. We generally do not make good, informed decisions when we're stressed or under pressure.

The other thing to think about is inheritance. If you want the value of the home to go to your children, whether a reverse mortgage is a good fit should be thought about in your estate planning.

Consider that the sales pitch for these products is often "well, in theory your home will increase in value as the interest is accrued, so you could actually not dip into your equity at all." Sure, that's possible, but we all know that "in theory" and "in reality" are two very different things. We've also seen housing prices slashed in many provinces.

The biggest criticism of reverse mortgages is the fees involved.

Besides PJ Wade, I also spoke with Keith Costello, President of the Canadian Institute of Financial Planners. He cautions against the high fees that exist with reverse mortgages including closing, appraisal, and legal and administrative costs. These are all upfront costs, so you have to be aware of the fact that these fees will be taken right off the initial amount they give you.

I called CHIP myself and asked about fees. First there's a fee of $1,495 that includes their legal and administration costs. Anyone arranging a reverse mortgage will also need to pay a lawyer, which typically costs from $300 to $600. And lastly, there's an appraisal, which also comes out of your pocket. They range from $175 to $400.

Also, the interest rate on reverse mortgages tends to be higher than what you would negotiate for a traditional mortgage with your banker (see rates below).

Finally, as with any loan, which is really what a reverse mortgage is, the responsible use of the money is really important. What if all the funds are used on vacations and other spending and the senior out lives their money? As a precaution, Mr. Costello suggests that, although you might be able to get up to 40% of the value of your home, take only what you need.

There are lots of other options that might exist, including a line of credit or traditional mortgage with your bank if you have the cash flow to cover the payments. Or you could consult a CFP who might be able to help you restructure your investments to free up cash flow.

When it comes to needing funds to renovate, a reverse mortgage might make sense if the money is being used to increase the overall value of the home and your enjoyment of living in it. But seniors should also remember that there might be some government grants out there that could pay or help them pay for things like windows and furnaces.

As with any product, there's no good or bad, it's what's good or bad for an individual's situation. For a senior who has no other option, desperately needs the money, has no other sources of income, and was adamant about staying in their home, this may be a viable option. But, having said that, the individual must keep in mind that with the high upfront costs and compounding interest, a reverse mortgage should be a last resort option, not the quick fix the commercials portray.

Additional background as of September 2009:

More CHIP facts:

- They have approximately 7,000 reverse mortgages on the books, totalling approx $833 million
- Their rates as of September 9, 2009, were higher than RBC's.
- As of September 9, 2009, CHIP's rates were 5.95% for a 1-year closed fixed term, and 7.50% for a 5-year, fixed closed term

Let's compare to RBC's 1-year and 5-year fixed rates (September 10, 2009, posted rates)

1 Year	3.70% open and 3.20% closed
5 Year	5.49% open and 4.19% closed

Recap

- Become familiar with current interest rates: they can significantly affect how much you'll pay in interest, the time it will take you to pay off your debt, and the return on your investments.
- Bank loans can be used for a variety of purchases and are paid back over a term with interest.
- Mortgages are a detailed, structured debt to be used towards the

purchase of a property or house.

- An alternative to a conventional mortgage is a secured line of credit, which allows the loan to be paid down and reused.
- Consider your options carefully: think through your down payment, term, and your amortization when trying to secure a mortgage.
- When in doubt, always crunch the numbers and be keenly aware of fees and fine print.
- Shop around and negotiate the best rate—this could be very beneficial in the long run.

An Interview with John DeGoey

I checked in with John DeGoey, financial professional and author of *Professional Financial Advisor II: How the Financial Services Industry Hides the Ugly Truth*, for his top money tips.

John's number one piece of advice was to not invest "one penny" into RRSPs, or any other investment for that matter, if you have high interest rate debt or non tax-deductible debt (debt that you can't deduct, such as that for a business or rental property). He noted the derailing of the credit gravy train in the US—how credit was being approved much too freely—should teach us Canadians that we need to focus first on debt reduction.

Second, John offered the sage advice that if you can't pay off your debt entirely, you should consolidate that debt in a forced principal banking product with an interest payment that is lower than your credit card interest rate. When I asked him if he sees clients in his practice with high credit card debt when they could flip it onto a low rate line of credit, he admitted not often, but it's still happening too often as far as he is concerned.

For example, he referred to someone who had $10,000 in credit card debt and a zero balance $50,000 line of credit (the latter having a much, much lower interest rate). The individual didn't want to move their credit card debt over to the line of credit for fear of racking up their credit card bill again. Obviously, it's not just the numbers that get and keep some people in financial trouble.

Lastly, John urged Canadians to focus more on their investments, the asset mix of their portfolios, and make sure to have advisors they trust look over their funds. John noted that the financial industry is guilty of asymmetrical information—advisors know more than their clients. John stresses that advisors too are human and that they might not always be guiding clients to make decisions in their best interest. He suggests that investors seek the advice of a Certified Financial Planner, and when circumstances warrant, those who are fee based. He concluded that even those pros aren't perfect, but that you'll get this best advice on the market by narrowing down the cream of the crop—the sales people vs. the pros. Look for an advisor who takes a holistic view towards clients' financial planning and who is not simply selling a product.

Chapter Seven

The Final Chapter

Quick Quiz

1. If you want to have a lump sum of funds available at death for your beneficiaries, which is the best alternative?

A: Mortgage insurance

B: Life insurance

C: Critical illness insurance

D: Disability insurance

2. Life insurance is tax exempt when paid out at death:

True ❑

False ❑

3. You don't need a power of attorney during your lifetime:

True ❑

False ❑

4. A will only kicks in at death:

True ❑

False ❑

5. Funerals can only be arranged and paid for when someone has passed away:

True ❑

False ❑

A number of years ago, a good friend of mine, Bernard, asked me for help when his mother passed away. It wasn't sudden, as she was in her mid-seventies and had been in the hospital making a superb recovery from a broken hip, but it was unexpected since she died from a hospital infection. As an only child with his father predeceasing his mother years before, the process of dealing with her funeral and finances seemed overwhelming.

I asked Bernard when his mom was in the hospital to have the "talk" with her. He refused: he thought that by bringing up what she wanted at her passing, she would think that he thought she was dying and it would hinder her recovery. Unfortunately, when she did pass, there were so many questions unanswered. Did she want to be cremated or buried and if the latter, where? Did she want a religious ceremony? She had attended church when her husband was alive, but had stopped. Was it because she didn't drive and all her friends that did had passed away years ago or did she stop going for a lack of interest? Was her house paid off? Did she have any debts or investments? Did she have any special mementoes that she wanted to gift to family or friends?

The only detail Bernard knew was where she banked, as he often drove her during errand runs. It was difficult even to convince the bank to open her safety deposit box where her will was located. Without the key it was tough to prove that in fact the will did name him as sole heir.

It was a grueling and emotional time for Bernard. He was officially an orphan and didn't have the faintest clue how to properly say goodbye to his mother and what her wishes would have been. If he had only had a brief talk with his mother, it wouldn't have spared his hurt and pain, but would have made the process of planning for her funeral (which Bernard took over ten days to do—most are organized within three or five days) and figuring out her finances much easier, to say the least.

Of all talks that you might have with your loved ones, bringing up the topic of death is certainly the most difficult. Well, not so much in my family. My mom and I have the total opposite relationship to Bernard and his mom. Coming from a very large (and rapidly aging) family, I can remember attending at least one if not several funerals each and every year since the time I was a small child. The "talk" is something my mom would discuss in bits with me after each ceremony. Plus, my mom updates me with details of her finale (as we call it), often. I know what songs she'd liked played, that she wants to be cremated, and the jewellery that she wants to leave and to whom. She changes her mind often and rings me with the updates.

For some, and I have to admit for me too, this talk can be morbid. Not everyone is as open as my mom and although it won't quell the loss when she's gone, I have a crystal clear picture of her final desires.

I encourage you to have the talk, even if those few minutes are excruciating, to find out the basics of what your loved ones want on their final day. As we all know, but prefer to ignore, death is something we'll all have to deal with eventually. Visit a list of my "tough" questions at www.kelleykeehn.com/themoneybook.html.

Your Documents

There are a number of documents that you need to have in place during your life, but only one deals with death. They're simple to complete yet amazingly difficult for many to get in order—death usually isn't on our Monday to-do list. These simple measures will save you and your family considerable grief and possibly thousands of dollars if they're in place during an emergency.

The major documents you should have in place are:

- Powers of attorney
- A living will or personal directives (called different things in different provinces)
- A will

The first two deal with matters while you're alive; only the will deals with your affairs after you've passed away. Each of these documents is relatively inexpensive and can be set up with most lawyers. If you have a complex estate, have dependents or a family member with a disability whom you care for, you might wish to choose an attorney who specializes in wills and estates. A basic will shouldn't cost more than $500 and a power of attorney, when done with a will, won't cost more than about $100. A basic power of attorney just for your banking can be set up at no cost at your bank, but keep in mind that it won't cover your other financial affairs. For that, you'd need a legal document with your lawyer. The same is true with your living will or personal directives. You can have a document on file of your wishes with your hospital or doctor, but if you travel or there's a chance you'll end up at a different hospital, it's best to have this drafted with your lawyer.

POWERS OF ATTORNEY (POAs)

A power of attorney allows a person whom you designate to have the ability to act on your behalf when dealing with your financial affairs. This designation is not to be taken lightly as you're essentially allowing someone, at any time, to act for you financially. Of course, you can cancel or change your power of attorneys at any time (as long as you're of sound mind). Why would you want a power of attorney set up? If you're married and have joint accounts with your spouse for example, it might not be necessary for you to have a regular power of attorney, but there might be cases where it would benefit you to do so. For someone who travels a great deal for work or for snowbirds, having a power of attorney is essential.

There's another type of power of attorney that I feel everyone should have, regardless of whether they have a regular POA or not. This second type deals with the event of mental incapacity only. This POA (often called an enduring POA) springs into effect in the event of a mental incapacity. Should that occur (from a skiing accident, delayed recovery from a surgery, Alzheimer's, etc.) a regular POA ceases to be legal. If one suffers a mental incapacity and this specific document doesn't exist, the person looking over your affairs would have to petition the court for guardianship. The entire process is lengthy and can be complex and very expensive, especially given that this document is simple and inexpensive.

When I still had my wealth management firm I had an 80-year-old client who travelled to Mexico. I urged him to get all of his documents in order (yes, at 80 and still travelling, you'd think he would have had them in order), but he dismissed my recommendation and headed south. He came down with a very severe disease and was flown home by air ambulance. He underwent two major surgeries and spent nearly a month in ICU. As you can imagine, he was unable to make any financial decisions regarding his massive real estate holdings during that time. His sister had a regular POA, but that was null and void once he was deemed mentally incapacitated by his doctors. He had a number of apartment buildings and other real estate. As the cheques came in from renters and the mortgage payments were due, his sister was unable to continue to act financially on his behalf. Not knowing if and when he'd be out of ICU and back to his old self, she was forced to start expensive proceedings to become his legal guardian. Thankfully, before much money was spent with on an attorney and legal proceedings, he came out of the hospital and was back to his old self. However, had he not recovered, it could have cost him thousands of dollars and considerable grief for his sister all because he didn't have this simple, low cost power of attorney in place.

If you go to a lawyer today, they'll almost certainly bring up the topic of POAs and living wills/personal directives. However, if you haven't updated your will in many years, you might not have this document in place.

LIVING WILLS/PERSONAL DIRECTIVES

This document deals with your health care wishes while you are alive. Again, not the easiest questions to ask yourself or a family member, but if you'd like your requests carried out, they need to be known by your health care team and family.

Before my step-dad passed away, and after his stroke, he lived with my mom. It was important to him that he not be resuscitated should something further happen to him. He had the documentation at his doctor's and with the hospital, but they also had the document on the fridge at their home. Why? When an ambulance arrives, their goal is to always resuscitate a person in need. Unless they can clearly see a legal document stating otherwise, they'll follow their mandate.

THE WILL

This document only kicks in at death. The will states how your assets will be divided and to whom. I won't get into the specifics of what happens if you don't have a will, but your estate, more than likely, won't be distributed as you'd wish. Also, if you have minor children or dependants, the will, among many other things, will detail who is to care and provide financially for your them.

Any banker, those in the financial industry or lawyers can tell you the old saying, "where there's a will, there's a relative." Every family hopes and might believe that they won't battle over assets at their death, but it's more likely that they will. Why not save your family the anguish and put your wishes in writing?

WHERE SHOULD YOU KEEP THESE DOCUMENTS?

With the living documents (the POAs and health care directives) you don't want these kept in your safety deposit box—how will someone access them when you need them? I would suggest keeping a copy of your POAs, healthcare directives, and will in your home and place the originals in your safety deposit box. Just ensure the person looking after your affairs knows where to find the key. Keep all important documents, such as your life insurance, in your safety deposit box or in a home safe. But again, make a list of these documents and consider keeping copies at home and another copy with your financial or legal representatives.

Insurance

There are a number of types of protection you should consider in your lifetime and to protect your estate and loved ones when you pass.

- Life insurance

- Mortgage insurance
- Disability insurance
- Critical illness insurance
- House insurance
- Automobile insurance
- Travel insurance.

I won't discuss the last three, as they're pretty self-explanatory. House and travel insurance are just smart options and auto, of course, is mandatory in every province.

LIFE INSURANCE

Life insurance is the type of coverage that you take out to financially help your loved ones after your passing and/or to cover your final expenses (funeral and/or debts). Life insurance may also be taken out for tax purposes. Life insurance proceeds are tax free and payable directly to your beneficiary (or multiple beneficiaries). For those with lots of debt, life insurance might make sense (if you can afford it) to cover those debts at death. For wealthy seniors, life insurance might not make sense because they already have the funds to self-insure. Life insurance costs vary greatly depending on your age, sex, health, recreational activities (are you a smoker? sky-diver?) and more. Obviously, the older you are and the poorer your health, the greater the cost of life insurance.

Life insurance is also used by some to provide tax-free cash to charities (a tax credit will result) or, if monies are to be gifted secretly. Because life insurance doesn't form part of the estate, it's not taxed and isn't subject to probate. Probate refers to a clearing of assets and debts before the court, which is necessary with estates of a certain size and made public. The details of this vary by province.

Mortgage insurance is sometimes thought of as life insurance, but it's not. It's paid out at death only to cover the remaining liability. There's credit card insurance as well, which is intended to pay out at death, to the credit card company for the balance owing (although the insurance can cover minimum payments during one's life when a qualified disability or job loss is suffered). Mortgage and credit card insurance is a premium that you pay to the lender, which would absolve your estate of debt at death. Some insurance agents criticize the cost of mortgage insurance over a personal policy. With the latter you have control over the costs and who will benefit. Be sure to shop around and examine the costs and options of both if you'd like to insure your debt.

When it comes to life insurance, there's a plethora of options on the market, but three main types exist:

1. *Term insurance.* This insurance is the least expensive of all, but the payment greatly increases at the end of each term and is usually bought to protect against a short-term need, such as covering the mortgage balance or other debts in the event of death. The premium rate is protected for a "term" of 10 or 20 years. At the expiry of that term, the insurance rate jumps substantially, so if insurance is needed for all of one's life, then one of the other options might be more suitable. Also, many term plans require an individual to re-qualify, health-wise, in order to renew. This requirement makes this plan less attractive for protecting long-term estate needs.

2. *T100.* This is a variance of the standard term. Here, the policy fee would cost more than straight term, but provide a guaranteed rate for life. It's less expensive than a "whole" life insurance policy, but still quite a bit costlier than Term 10 for example.

3. *Whole life.* These policies used to be the only option on the market many years ago. You might have heard the "buy term and invest the rest" phrase from years ago, however, whole life can be a viable option for the right individual. The premium cost factors in an investment element as well, which can be a benefit later in the policy life. Think of it like a T100—rates remain the same for life, but with an investment element (which many in the financial industry criticize for being too costly).

The investment portion of the policy can be separate from the insurance, or can be a return of premium (you pay more in the early years and the insurance company returns some of that extra later on). Whole life policies can be quite complex with many elements within it. Ensure you always shop around and get a second opinion when purchasing any life insurance.

There's no right or wrong insurance option on the market. What you should consider is whether that product suits your specific needs. Ask yourself how much coverage do you need? What's your age, health, and how long do you need it to be in place? The second question is do you need insurance at all and if so, how much? There are many excellent insurance agents out there, but remember, their job is to sell you insurance. If possible, shop their quotes around to your financial advisor or fee-only CFP to ensure you're not under- or over-insured.

You'll find a number of useful insurance calculators that will let you play around with the costs of different types of plans and amounts on my website at www.kelleykeehn.com/themoneybook.html.

DISABILITY INSURANCE

This type of insurance covers the lost income you might suffer due to a disability. These policies vary widely and the premiums and coverage are based on your age, sex, type of job, and payout/disability. You may have a policy at your place of employment. If you don't and are interested, ensure you shop around and clearly understand the fine print. These policies can be expensive if you want all of the bells and whistles. And some people are extremely shocked when it's time to make a claim and their particular situation or disability is denied. Some policies will not pay out if you can do any type of work, even if it's work you wouldn't normally do (i.e., a neurosurgeon with the most basic policy might not be paid anything if she could do any other type of work for example).

CRITICAL ILLNESS (CI) INSURANCE

A somewhat newer player on the market (only about 20 years old) is critical illness. As the name suggests, it pays a lump sum benefit in the event of a major, covered illness. Unlike disability insurance that would pay out a monthly benefit (likely after a waiting period), CI pays out immediately if the illness is covered by the policy. Each company differs as to what is covered, but typically illnesses and diseases covered by CI insurance may include: cancer, heart attack, stroke, blindness, MS, Alzheimer's, and more. As you can imagine, this type of insurance can be quite expensive as you age and the possibility of illness increases.

Tough End of Life Questions

To continue the macabre but necessary discussion about preparing and protecting ourselves and our loved ones after our deaths, I've assembled the top tough questions to ask yourself, your spouse, your parents, and siblings. There is no good time to really ask these questions, but they've got to be asked and ideally when someone is in good health.

I think the first important question for your parents, spouse and family is, what do you want done with your remains? Is it cremation? If so, where would you like your ashes spread, fully intact in one container, divided, or buried? (Most places offer the large urn and a little one for the fireplace.)

Is it burial? If so, where? Do you have a plot already purchased?

The other thing you need to take into account is religion—would you like a minister? If so, what denomination? Would you like a prayer service, wake, a non-religious gathering, or something else?

WHAT ABOUT WHEN IT COMES TO HEALTH CARE?

You need to look at living wills and personal directives. If there is one in place, people need to know where to find it and know which hospital to deal with. Who's the family doctor? It's amazing how many adult children don't know this about their own parents.

WHAT ARE SOME OF THE TOUGH QUESTIONS THAT COME WITH PERSONAL DIRECTIVES?

Basically, what type of care and when would you like it administered during a time of illness. Do you want to be resuscitated, for example? If the answer is no, it needs to be known by all family members. If 911 is called, the paramedics will always try to resuscitate, so if you don't want that, a document should be posted on the fridge in plain site.

While it seems that living wills and personal directives are more of a senior's issue, you never know what can happen and when. These are issues for every age group.

People should talk to their loved ones about things like organ donation too. Your family should know what you want, and you should know what family members would like to do.

There are also decisions to be made regarding Last Rites, anointing, and prayer. At a time of sickness, would you like someone called for prayer and if so, what type (denomination, minister, anyone)?

WHAT ABOUT LEGAL ISSUES? WHAT QUESTIONS SHOULD YOU BE ASKING?

Everyone should have an enduring power of attorney. This is different from a regular power of attorney. Say that you travel a great deal and have someone look after your financial affairs while you're away. In the event of mental incapacity, even if only for a short while, a regular power of attorney would cease to be legal. This is where an "enduring" power of attorney is needed. It only takes effect during a mental incapacity. Please secure your own legal advice, as each province and situation may be different.

Whom would you like to make these decisions (financial and otherwise) in the event of incapacity? This person should be informed of the location of your will (if there is one). That leads us to the safety deposit box. If there is one, where are the keys kept and where is the box itself?

Lastly, you'll want to consider special gifts. Do you have any that are essential to pass on? Where are your pictures for the ceremony or obituary?

For a complete checklist of tough questions to ask (you just have to do it once and record it), visit www.kelleykeehn.com/themoneybook.html. Ensure that loved ones know where the checklist is kept.

Funeral Planning: Tough Discussions

Obviously, funeral planning, and simply striking a conversation, can be extremely emotional and difficult. Most individuals will only go through the process of planning a funeral once or twice in their lives and that's what the industry is counting on. There are some great folks out there in the biz, but many count on your not knowing what you're doing and overspending to ward off feelings of guilt. Since it's such a quick process—usually just a few days after death—and so stressful, people don't always make the best decisions.

Keep in mind that funeral directors are not clergy, even though some people trust them implicitly. They're in the business to make money. You do not have to buy the whole bundle of services.

What does the average funeral cost?

I went to three different places in my city to get examples of pricing and info. I was told that the average is $4,000–$6,000, but that number can vary widely. It all depends on the service, closed or open casket (the latter costs much more), and whether the person chooses cremation or burial. According to AARP, a not-for-profit advocacy association for those 50 and over, funeral and burial costs can easily reach as much as $10,000. Flowers, obituary notices, burial liners or vaults, limousines, acknowledgement cards—they all add up to be major expenses—and if you choose burial, the costs continue to rise.

What's the cost difference for burial?

A wood casket might run $250 while the "Cadillac" of caskets could be as high as $35,000. The average is around $3,500–$5,500. You can also rent one for cremation or viewing. The price for the actual plot and all that's required along with it will also add from about $1,700 (at a city cemetery) and upwards to the bill. That's not factoring in the headstone, of course.

A funeral provider may not refuse or charge a fee to handle a casket you bought elsewhere.

With burial comes embalming, something that is encouraged, but actually not a necessity in all cases. Embalming is rarely required when the person will be buried within 24 to 48 hours.

Another thing to know is that sealed caskets cannot preserve a body. Sealed caskets cost hundreds of dollars more than unsealed caskets.

WHAT KIND OF COSTS COME WITH CREMATION?

Cremation can be less expensive than a burial and if there's no viewing, even less. Cremation with pick-up and no service will run about $1,500–$2,000. But you may still have costs, like an obituary, which averages $300–$500 per day.

WHAT QUESTIONS SHOULD YOU ASK WHEN FUNERAL PLANNING?

I know most people wouldn't think of negotiating when funeral planning, but as with any business, a price isn't always a price. And with a little advance thinking about it, I hope everyone can make better and less emotional decisions. After all, it can be an extremely costly event. Funeral services are one of the largest purchases consumers make, right up there with a car and a house.

Second, if a parent, for example, is in long-term care at a non-hospital facility, you need to make plans ahead. I know it's terribly morbid, but if the family is on vacation, these places don't have a morgue and need to address deaths quickly. If they have to make the decision, it might cost you hundreds of extra dollars.

Paying for the End

LET'S SAY YOU'RE RELYING ON CPP TO PAY FOR A FUNERAL. HOW MUCH WILL IT COVER?

You need to keep in mind is that if a person didn't pay into CPP (the Canada Pension Plan) their entire working career, they might receive less than the $2,500 maximum death benefit.

CAN YOU TALK TO THE FUNERAL HOME ABOUT A PAYMENT PLAN?

With many homes, yes, you can talk to the funeral home about a payment plan. They don't advertise it, but most will wait to receive the CPP benefit $2,500 after all the final tax returns have been filed and probate's been settled, especially if it is a matter of not having liquid funds. (This could occur if there's a large asset, such as a home, that takes time to liquidate.)

PREPAID AND PRE-ARRANGED FUNERALS

A lot of people look at prepaid and pre-arranged funerals. First of all, what are the important differences between prepaid and pre-arranged?

Pre-arranged is just that: you've met with a funeral home and documented what you'd like, but you haven't necessarily paid. Prepaid is where you've made the arrangements and prepaid via life insurance, or another form of payment.

What are the advantages of a prepaid funeral?

1. *Growth isn't taxable.* As long as the expenses incurred are for eligible funeral expenses as defined by the Canadian Income Tax Act, the growth is non-taxable.
2. *It's much easier to think rationally when not grieving.* It's difficult to think clearly while making so many decisions within days of losing someone. Being frugal is often the furthest thing on someone's mind in the aftermath of death. It's simply easier to make those difficult decisions while not under so much stress.
3. *Your wishes are honoured.* Perhaps there are certain songs you'd like played, traditions to be adhered to, a specific burial location, and more.
4. *It's easy to get.* Buying life insurance for someone in their 80s with major health issues is a challenge. Prepaid funerals don't require a health screening or age limit to qualify.

WHAT ARE THE DRAWBACKS OF A PREPAID FUNERAL?

1. *They aren't a good investment.* The interest they generate is minimal. The plan contributor has little control over where or how the money is invested.

2. *There are scams out there.* You will need to:
   - Ensure the funds are held either in an income trust or as a part of an insurance policy at a recognized Canadian financial institution covered under the CDIC (Canada Deposit Insurance Corporation).
   - Ensure the funeral home is a licensed funeral provider and is licensed under the pre-arranged funeral legislation in your province.
   - Confirm with the funeral home that you can transfer your pre-paid arrangement anywhere in Canada.
   - Keep track of the policy and let your family know where it is.

OVERALL, IS PRE-PAYING A GOOD IDEA?

I don't think so. If you're looking for tax-free growth and think you have a few years, the money would best be put in a TFSA (Tax Free Savings Account). At least that way, you'd still have control over how the money is invested and it would be there when needed. You can still pre-arrange your funeral so that your wishes are carried out how you'd like without paying for it.

Lastly, if you have a loved one in assisted living of any type, you need to let that facility know your wishes well in advance.

Recap

- Make an appointment today with a lawyer (and encourage your spouse and family to do the same) to ensure that your will, powers of attorney, and living will/personal directives are up to date.
- Have a tough talk with loved ones and be sure to document your wishes and share that document with others.
- Make a checklist of where important documents are located.
- Create a binder listing all professionals you deal with, their contact numbers, and the policy or account numbers of bank and

investment accounts, life insurance policies, and more. It's a good idea to include an approximate net worth statement of assets and debts.

- Make sure the person whom you've elected as executor or to handle your affairs if something were to happen to you knows where your safety deposit key and documents are located.
- Visit my website at www.kelleykeehn.com/themoneybook.html for a list of top tough questions to ask and your binder checklist.

As explained throughout this book, the nature of this guide is to provide you with a basic understanding of a variety of financial concepts. However, estate planning is the most complex of all and requires the most advanced planning to ensure that your wishes are honoured, funds are available to dependents and loved ones, and taxation is fully understood. If you're looking to better understand the complexities of estate planning, consider further research on:

- Choosing an executor
- Trusts
- Spousal prescribed loans
- Taxation at death
- Charitable gifting
- Cottages and out of country real estate
- Succession planning

Conclusion

So you made it through the wild adventures of personal finance. This gives you the knowledge, and the power, to make some informed choices about your finances. It is time for you to create a little prosperity.

Take some time to reflect on WHY achieving financial security is important to you. What does it mean for you? For your family? For your future? Maybe the first things that come to mind are trips, a new car or truck, or those cute shoes you saw—which may all be true—however, I am also thinking about the deeper reason you might want financial knowledge, whether it is security, being able to provide for your aging parents, to start a family, buy your first property, or being able to do whatever your mind can come up with during retirement.

The next step is to create long- and short-term goals. What do you want to accomplish with your personal finances in the next six months? Year? Five years? Twenty years?

Then, create an action plan. Take the knowledge you learned from *The Money Book* and challenge yourself to get your money working for you, instead of the other way around. Create a list of bills, start to review your credit card statements, purchase your credit report, and make an appointment to meet with a financial planner. These are small steps, but they will help you reach your financial goals.

I know it hasn't been the most exciting or sexy journey getting through this book (even though some of the scams can be titillating). My sincere hope is that you feel a little more empowered and able to protect yourself financially in the future after working through this book. I encourage you to visit my website at www.kelleykeehn.com/themoneybook.html for updated material.

Now is the best time to start moving towards your goals. Go live life prosperously!

Acknowledgments

"They" (whoever they are) say it takes a village to raise a child. Well, it also takes a gaggle of support to assist in producing a book that I then get most of the credit for (wrongly, of course).

It would equally take a book to list all of those who, over the years, have allowed me to produce this book along with my others. I owe a great debt to many and hope the beneficiaries of this book are more financially educated Canadians.

My heartfelt thanks to Mike O'Connor, Gillian Rodgerson, and Insomniac Press for producing another one of my books. To my brilliant and very patient editor, Gillian Urbankiewicz, for making my writing readable and as palatable as a financial book can possibly be. To Lisa Bélanger for initiating this project and believing in financial literacy as much as I do. To Mark Dickey and the Alberta Securities Commission for allowing me to include their very valuable information outlined in Chapter Four. To Neel Roberts, President of PTC Canada, for his assistance with bouncing calculations and numbers back and forth.

And of course, thank you to my family and friends (both two and furry four-legged) for their support, guidance, and long-suffering in my near disappearance from their lives to complete this manuscript. And utmost appreciation to my husband Wyatt for his sacrifices in allowing me to focus on this project for the last half year.

Lastly, to you my reader, I extend my most sincere and humble thanks. It is because of you and your feedback, comments, and desire to be financially free that this book came into fruition. I hope *The Money Book* will be your first step to a solid financial foundation. As always, I'd love to hear from you. Please email me at wealth@kelleykeehn.com.

To your prosperity,
Kelley

Quick Quiz Answer Key

CHAPTER ONE

1. How many credit cards should you have?

There isn't a magic number and it does depend on your lifestyle. (Do you travel a great deal or would having extra cards be a temptation to spend?) Ideally, you should have at least two cards and one with a zero balance, should something happen to the first.

2. Your mortgage payment history is listed on your credit report.

Generally in Canada, it is not.

3. How often should you check your credit report?

This was sort of a trick question. A said, "Never—it hurts your score," which is totally false. You can check your score as many times as you want since your own inquiries count as a "soft" inquiry and don't affect your score. Monthly is likely overkill, but I would suggest at least once or twice a year.

4. You should have a low-limit card for making internet purchases.

It's not a bad idea, but remember, you're 100% protected by VISA and MasterCard. Plus, I've had my high-limit credit card number stolen and never used that card online. Remember, a server at a restaurant or a clerk with a photographic memory can misuse your number, not just fraudulent merchants on the internet.

5. If you have a poor credit score, there's not much you can do for six years.

That would be false. As we examined in Chapter One, there's a great deal you can do to improve your score such as keeping your account balances low, not going "over" limit, paying your credit card on time every month, and not seeking new credit.

Chapter Two:

1. You don't need to review your credit card statements with VISA and MasterCard because you're 100% protected against fraudulent purchases.

This is another trick question. The latter is true, that you're 100% protected, but you should still carefully check your statements for incorrect purchases along with fraudulent ones. Plus, it's a good idea to review your spending monthly anyway!

2. If fraud occurs with your debit card, you're not protected.

You're well aware by now that the answer is false.

3. It's a good idea not to have savings accounts with large amounts linked to your debit card.

It is a good idea, but because you're also protected by the major six banks (and likely the rest as well) against debit card theft, it's not essential.

4. Identity theft isn't much of an issue here in Canada.

I know that you know that one is false!

5. When paying with your credit card, there's nothing wrong with showing your ID when a merchant asks.

False, as you learned, it could in some instances allow a would-be identity thief to have just about all the information needed to apply for credit in your name.

CHAPTER THREE:

1. All mutual funds are taxed the same.

False. Just as individual investments are taxed differently, so are mutual funds.

2. To be truly diversified, you should have what percentage of your portfolio in stocks?

The correct answer was D. It depends on a number of factors such as your age, experience dealing with investments, net worth, your risk tolerance, and more.

3. Your principal residence is considered a very safe investment.

This is a trick question. There are not too many "very" safe investments on the market. You also learned in this chapter that although your home is an asset, unless you plan to sell your home to fund your retirement, it's not an investment. Since you have to live somewhere, however, it's a great asset to have.

4. There's absolutely no risk investing in a GIC (Guaranteed Investment Certificate) at your bank.

Sort of true. Yes, you're guaranteed your principal plus interest, however, if rates increase and you're locked-in to a lower rate, you're exposed to interest rate risk. Plus, if rates do increase from when you locked in, it means that inflation has also increased, therefore you'd also be exposed to inflation risk—not earning more than inflation after tax.

5. In Canada, you get a tax deduction on the interest you pay for your principal residence, but don't get taxed when you sell it.

If you said "sort of true" you were just about right! The first part is wrong; you do not get a tax deduction, but you also don't have to pay tax when you sell it.

CHAPTER FOUR:

1. A guaranteed return of 10% is reasonable to expect.

In today's low interest rate environment, if someone is guaranteeing you 10%, you'd better run! They might pay you 10% in the short-term or periodically, but then your principal will be at great risk.

2. Research of an investment is the responsibility of:

A and D—you and your financial professional. Government agencies might regulate investments, but they don't research them.

3. If you've been with your financial advisor for five years or more, you don't need to check up on their credentials.

As you learned, Earl Jones' clients were with him for years and never questioned him. It's a good idea to check with the organizations outlined in Chapter Four to ensure your financial professional is still in good standing; once every year would be prudent.

4. You should always request investment specifics in writing, even from those you know and trust.

True. Any reputable professional offering any type of investment would have no issue with such a request.

5. If an investment has a short window of time to get in, you should:

All were correct except the first one. Never invest immediately unless you've done all of your research and clearly understand every aspect of an investment.

CHAPTER FIVE:

1. RRSPs and RRIFs are actual investments.
As you learned, this is false. They're simply tax shelters or "garages"; you still need to fill them with investments or "cars."

2. Interest on an RRSP loan is tax deductible.
False. Because you get a tax deduction for investing in an RRSP, you don't get a tax break if you take out a loan to invest.

3. A Tax-Free Savings Account is best suited for investors who are:
D was the correct answer. A TFSA could suit just about anyone. Although investment funds might be better suited in an RRSP or used for paying down debt, remember that a TFSA is just another shelter, not an investment in itself.

4. Non-registered investments grow tax free.
Of course, false.

5. Investments producing capital gains, interest income, or dividends are all taxed at the same rate.
I know you know that this one is also false!

CHAPTER SIX:

1. If interest rates are low and starting to rise, the economy should expect to:
The answer would be A. The economy would slowly start to tighten as rates increased because as it becomes more expensive to borrow

for purchases like cars and homes, people stop buying as much, and that can mean job cuts and fears of unemployment and thus the cycle moves.

2. Your credit score is the only thing that matters when applying for a mortgage:

False. Your income, net-worth, purchase price, and more matter when applying for a mortgage.

3. You can negotiate the rate of your mortgage with your prospective lender.

Absolutely!

4. Once you've decided on an amortization, there's nothing you can do to reduce it.

False. As you learned, you can change your amortization by increasing your monthly payments or by making annual lump sum payments on the principal.

5. In the long-term, a variable rate mortgage will generally cost less than a comparable fixed rate mortgage over, say, a 25-year amortization.

True

CHAPTER SEVEN:

1. If you want to have a lump sum of funds available at death for your beneficiaries, which is the best alternative?

B—Life insurance would be the correct answer.

2. Life insurance is tax exempt when paid out at death:

True.

3. You don't need a power of attorney during your lifetime:

False. As you learned, there are many instances when you might need a POA during your lifetime. Also, don't forget that there are various with types of POAs.

4. A will only kicks in at death:

True.

5. Funerals can only be arranged and paid for when someone has passed away:

False. You can pre-arrange and/or pre-pay for a funeral during your lifetime.

Index

About the Authors

KELLEY KEEHN

Kelley Keehn is a financial expert, speaker, media personality and author of seven books, including *She Inc., The Woman's Guide to Money* and *The Prosperity Factor for Kids*. Kelley uncovers the "inner games" we play surrounding wealth. As a former financial professional for over a decade, she's witnessed first-hand the problems individuals have with money and has developed a number of fun and practical guides to making changes to our money mindsets at a fundamental level. Kelley discovered that whether someone had a billion in the bank or is a million in the hole, everyone has money problems!

Kelley is a regularly sought-after media guest, appearing on TV and radio around the globe and has had many regular columns and published articles. In November 2009, she was quoted in Oprah's *O Magazine*. She was a regular contributor for CNBC (New York), a weekly columnist with *CBC Radio Active*, a weekly nationally syndicated financial columnist with CBC radio, a weekly panellist for Alberta Primetime's money panel, and a regular guest on CTV.

Today she is proud to be the host of *Burn My Mortgage*, which aired a full season in the fall of 2010 and early 2011 on the W Network. She travels across the country speaking for some of Canada's largest corporations and is a weekly contributor to the *Globe and Mail* and AOL's *WalletPop Canada*.

LISA BÉLANGER

Lisa Bélanger completed her undergraduate degree in Human Kinetics with Honours at St. Francis Xavier University, Antigonish, Nova Scotia. She was recently granted her Masters in Science and is currently working on her doctorate at the University of Alberta. She is studying Behaviour Medicine, the study of behaviour change. While the primary focus of her research is the effect of physical activity on cancer survivors, her interests also extend to how behavioural theories can be applied to different fields, including personal finance.

Lisa is also a visionary and macro thinker who caught Kelley's attention when she mentioned a possible collaboration on a book. Lisa and Kelley continue to brainstorm and execute projects together.